POPPIES

POPPIES

ODYSSEY OF AN OPIUM EATER

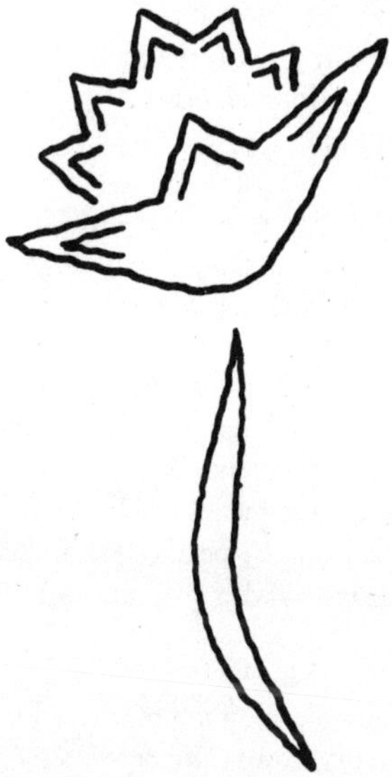

ERIC DETZER

Mercury House, Incorporated
San Francisco

Published in the United States by
Mercury House
San Francisco, California

Distributed to the trade by
Kampmann & Company, Inc.
New York, New York

Manufactured in the United States of America

Library of Congress Cataloging-in-Publication Data
Detzer, Eric, 1948–
Poppies : odyssey of an opium eater / Eric Detzer.
p. cm.
ISBN 0–916515–30–3 : $8.95
1. Detzer, Eric, 1948–. 2. Narcotic addicts — United States — Biography. 3. Drug abuse counselors — United States — Biography. 4. Opium habit — United States — Case studies. I. Title.
HV5805.D47A3 1988
362.2'93 — dc19 87–28746
[B] CIP

for
Arthur M. Corning
1911–1987

Now for something with poison in it . . .

–THE WICKED WITCH OF THE WEST

1

Walpurgis Night

I come from a long line of people who don't know what to do with their hands. To a one, we are all reluctant to simply let our hands hang until they are needed. We twine our fingers, rub our palms, and pick at whatever is available. Once, when I had to make a particularly long and complicated confession to my mother, she was literally reduced to sitting on her hands in order to prevent them from becoming a distraction. I myself have a well-choreographed little dance I do with my fingers whenever I become excited.

I'm watching my hands tonight as they twitch and tremble. Tonight, November 1, 1985, is a night to dance the fingers. Tonight, God help me, I am going to kick.

No more putting it off. I've said I was going to do it for months. I've known I needed to do it for years. My stash of opium is completely gone. Old Dr. Higgins is burned down; he will never write for me again. It would take some doing to get another source going and I don't have time before withdrawal begins. I could probably look up Strake and buy a hit, but I'd only be fixed for one day and would be a hundred dollars poorer. Then I'd be sick again. No, there's no reasonable way to make a connection tonight.

Besides—I've had enough.

I remember when I was young. I used to sit in the bathtub in the morning and think of all the things I had to do that day. I would map out my day as I scrubbed my body. As each new thing occurred to me I would feel a little tingle of excitement until I would eventually come bounding out of the tub, filled with energy and ready to take on a new day. That's the way I want to feel again. The past few years I have greeted each day with such an overwhelming sense of sadness and fear that I rarely even want to get out of bed, let alone bathe. That's no way to live. That's not living. That's stupid. Dance away, little fingers. Tonight is the beginning of my new life!

★

(Jesus. Just fell asleep for a few minutes, maybe half an hour. Woke up with my shirt soaked in sweat. It's really starting. I hope I'm ready because there's no turning back now. Jesus.)

★

There is nothing to fucking *do* at four o'clock in the morning. I slept a while, what they call "yen sleep," a few moments of unconsciousness characteristic of early withdrawal. I dreamed I was on a slave ship chained to an oar. I woke up on the floor; I'd slipped out of the chair I was sitting in. Now there's another cigarette burn in the carpet. Actually I feel all right, considering. If it doesn't get too much worse than this I'm pretty sure I'll be okay. Except what is there to do at four o'clock in the morning.

You know, I hate pharmacists. Doctors are just dumb. If they write, they're dumb for believing the story. If they don't write, they're dumb for *not* believing the story. But pharmacists are evil. They have a special ability to see right through a dope fiend. They can tell instantly, just by looking at a prescription, whether it was written in response to a story you concocted. They give you these withering looks that say, "I know what you're up to, you son-of-a-bitch." They're especially bad at refill time. They know it's way too soon, and they don't for one minute believe you accidentally dropped them in the toilet while struggling with the childproof container. You put your bottle on the counter; he can feel your riveting stare. He turns. He either moves toward the bottle or toward the phone to call the doctor. If he calls, you can kiss your stuff good-bye. If he fills it, he only does it so you'll get your scumbag, junkie self out of his nice, clean pharmacy. There's nothing a pharmacist would enjoy more than a whole stage full of sick junkies, writhing and squirming in agony. "Bravo, bravo!" he'd yell, and clap his hands in delight. If I ever get off narcotics I'm never going to speak to a pharmacist again as long as I live.

Ahh . . . I don't feel very good. The window is open but I'm burning up. If I move closer to the window I get chilled, though. Seems my comfort range is getting pretty narrow. I keep sneezing and I'm rubbing my nose raw trying to keep the snot from building up in my mustache. I may be a miserable, strung-out excuse for a human being, but I've got my pride. I will not sit here, even at four in the morning, with snot on my face. Maybe if I took a hot bath my legs would stop aching for a while. Yeah, that's it. I'll take a hot bath, change my clothes, and then make coffee. It'll be dawn soon. I'll get myself cleaned up, have a cup of coffee, and take a walk. I need some exercise. I've been sitting in this same chair for hours. I'll have another cigarette and then do it. Jesus, I feel terrible.

It's more comfortable in here now that I've put the fan on. The bath helped for a while, though the effect is wearing off It's better being clean. In the hum of the fan it seems as though I can hear music playing. Hmmm, hmmm. Yeah, "Somewhere over the Rainbow." God, it's such a sad song. I never realized what a sad one it is. Jesus, I'm starting to cry. This is weird.

★

We go back a long way, the poppy and I. Nineteen years now since my first hit. I was nineteen and a member of the generation that brought heroin out of the ghetto and into the suburbs. I was one of those early pioneers who ventured into the bowels of Harlem, looking for that magic stuff we had heard about only in whispers. God, I must have looked ridiculous. But my money was as green as anybody's, even if I did carry it in my wallet instead of my sock. I was with a guy named Bert whom I'd only recently met and thoroughly disliked. We copped on the corner of 125th and Lex, then rode the subway back to his place on 11th between A and B. In those days a half-load was quite a bit of stuff, so Bert, his friend Alley Boy, and I were able to get off (at my expense, of course). I didn't throw up and I didn't show my terror of the dirty little needle with the point bent back from being dropped on the floor. To me it was a wonderful, exciting adventure into never-never land, which I assumed I'd never do again. Ha, ha, ha. Never, never, never. Shit.

I bought (I mean copped) another half-load and brought it back to New England where I was in college. I wanted to impress the girl who would later become my wife; the girl (I mean woman) who is asleep in the next room right now, who thinks I am making too much of a fuss over this kicking business. She *was* duly impressed and even asked me to move in with her. She had dropped out of school already, as was the fashion of the day. I would follow suit in a few months. A lot of toxin has passed through my liver since that day.

★

It's raining now. When Lewis and Clark came to western Washington they recorded in their journal that they had entered a "living hell." It rained on them for weeks without a break. Their Indian guides and laborers died from colds they caught from the white explorers, illnesses to which they had no immunities. It rained and it rained. It's still raining. I don't know if I'd call it a "living hell" out there, but it is raining and it's fucked as far as I'm concerned. I'm a southwesterner. What am I doing in this great, green sponge?

Lately I think about the weather almost obsessively. I don't remember doing that before. Especially when I feel sad, I miss the Southwest. I remember juniper, and there must have been piñon, too. Manzanita, mallow, and Indian paint brush blooming in the spring. Birch, alder, and aspen down by Oak Creek in the shadow of the red rocks. Dusty—everything was dusty. Rutted back roads, quail bobbing around. I used to like to get up early and sit out on a rock, before the fucking sun would get too hot. It seems funny to me that I should miss all that now. All I ever wanted to do was leave that goddamn desert when I lived there. Washington, with all its lush green, seemed like a paradise to me then.

I should either shut that damn fan off or put on the TV or something to cover the sound it makes. I keep hearing all these sad songs coming out of it. Now it seems as if I can hear "Amazing Grace," very faint, very far away. Tears keep welling up in my eyes as I try to hear the music; then my nose dumps even more snot on my mustache. I can feel my cough reflex beginning to come back. It's like several hundred ants are digging in for the winter in the back of my throat. When I cough, I gag; when I cough hard, I throw up. Sometimes, if I vomit with solid conviction, I get a rush of diarrhea in my shorts. This is starting to get disgusting.

The rain is letting up and it's beginning to get light.

⋆

The people who are just starting to use drugs now, those who are the same age as I was on 11th between A and B, consider me middle-aged. And I guess I am. If I die at the same age as my father and grandfather, I am, in my mid-thirties, at the very midpoint in my life. Isn't that middle-aged?

In the 1940s, the era in which I entered this world, pregnancy was regarded more or less as an illness by the medical profession. My mother entered the hospital with much the same attitude as a person on the eve of an appendectomy. She packed enough cold cream and nightgowns for a week, knowing she would be staying at least that long. Her contractions, mild and irregular on admission, became urgent within twenty minutes after signing the Blue Cross forms, and I sailed into the doctor's hands one hour later. My mother, of course, was unaware of the speed of my birth, being totally unconscious at the time. In those days, the medical profession saw delivery as major surgery. Even in swift, uncomplicated births such as mine, anesthesia was routinely administered. I was born small and jaundiced (and probably loaded from the dope that had managed to cross the placental barrier), so was whisked away by the nurses and put under lights. My mother did not see me for forty-eight hours.

Luckily, my jaundiced condition passed almost as rapidly as my mother's anesthetic stupor. I was brought to her at feeding time, so for the first week our time together was limited. My mother had had three children before me and, though she felt just fine, she allowed the doctors to convince her that something traumatic and perhaps terrible had happened to her. She did enjoy the time away from the fights and runny noses of my three siblings, though a gnawing sense of guilt kept her from enjoying that respite as much as she might. My father visited twice, but he felt awkward and in the way and left before his time was up.

My early years in the Phoenix suburbs are right out of the Dick and Jane books, which would eventually teach me to read. These books have been much maligned lately because minority kids can't "relate to" the characters. But I could. They described me, my family, my home.

Dick and Jane go to the grocery store; Dick and Jane go to the zoo. (Dick does ninety days in the county jail for boosting cigarettes from a Seven-Eleven, ha ha.)

★

I think it was a mistake to drink coffee. My hands are trembling and I think it's made the runs worse. I can hear Sarah waking up. Maybe it will be good to have some company, get my mind off myself for a while, even if she doesn't really understand what I'm going through. "If you're getting too strung out," she said last week, "why don't you stop doing it?"

"It's not that easy," I said. "You don't know what it's like. I can't just stop, say 'Okay, that's it, I've had enough' and just *stop*. I mean, Christ, I'm hooked on the stuff, hooked. I can't just *stop*."

"Why not?" she asked.

"Because I'm *hooked!*" I moaned. "Hooked. I'll have to go through withdrawal. I don't know if I can stand it."

"Oh for Christsakes," she quipped. "Don't be so dramatic, bubaleh. You've done it before. Mostly it's all in your head. It'll be as bad as you decide it's going to be. Just keep busy. Don't sit around and stew in your own juices. Hey, you've got snot on your mustache."

"Maybe so, maybe so," I said. "Maybe it is in my head. But my head is terrified. Every time I go through it it's worse. I just don't think I can stand it." I knew I was babbling nonsense and that she was only half listening. She's never felt that overpowering obsession that takes over a dope fiend's consciousness. She's never tried to fight the compulsion to dash out the door and make a connection, no matter what the consequences. She's never been hooked; not like I am.

"Well, if you can't stand it, don't kick," she remarked logically. "Keep on using."

"I can't," I said. "This isn't living. This is bullshit. I have to stop."

"Eric, listen," she said, "you've been going through this since 1968. Sixteen years. Every few months you tell me you're strung out again and have to go through withdrawal. You drag yourself around the house for a couple of weeks, then things go back to normal. And just when I think I can finally relax, wham!! You make your big 'I'm hooked' announcement again. I know you think I'm being insensitive, but, Christ, how much of this can a person take?"

"All I'm asking is that you try to understand what I'm going through," I said, but that wasn't absolutely true. What I really wanted from her was sympathy and she knew it.

"I'm all out of sympathy, bubaleh," she said. "I know it's different for you than it is for me. You get much more hung up on stuff than I do. But there comes a point where I have to say you're going to do what you do, and nothing I say is going to change that. I've got to protect myself. The wash still has to be done, the strawberries still have to be hoed, whether you're high, clean, or kicking."

So many of our conversations about my drug use go this way. I am never able to say directly what I am feeling. If my habit was costing great sums of money, she would be the first to insist that I put it down. If my health was deteriorating, she would certainly see that as a reason to stop. How can I explain to her how I feel, that I have this growing sense of wrongness about myself? Narcotic drugs poison the spirit and my spirit has been so battered and anesthetized that most of the time I don't feel human. Without that spirit I am a cardboard piece of backdrop scenery who can't hold his eyes open, can't shit, and can't even get a hard-on four days out of five.

It's raining again. This will knock most of the remaining yellow leaves from the cottonwoods. It will turn the harvested pea fields to brown soup. Migrating mallards sometimes swim in the pools left by the incessant rain. I have the sense that moss is beginning to grow on my back. Somehow it never seemed quite as wet when we lived down in Seattle, before we decided to move to the farm country for "the good life."

*

I can never keep up on drug addict slang, and since I quit hanging out with drug users, I haven't tried. It changes with the passage of time, and it varies so much regionally that a Kansas City dope fiend can hardly talk to a Miami dope fiend. An old fossil like me, who's been around for nearly two decades, simply can't stay hip (or whatever the word is today). But a person must think in language and there are no words to describe feelings associated with drug use, so I've had to invent my own slang.

I think of the various conditions of the drug addict as Houses.

When you're addicted to opiates you live in the Monkey House. This comes from the old dope fiend saying, "monkey on my back," an incredibly apt expression. Think of what it would be like if, literally, there was a live monkey who rode around on your back all day. You get up in the morning and the first order of business has to be to feed that damn monkey. A hungry monkey would hit and scream and bite and choke you. It would be absolutely impossible to ignore. So you feed it. And the more you feed it, the more docile it becomes. So you feed it as much as you possibly can. But even if it's completely sated, you still have to lug it around all day, knowing it's going to be hungry again tomorrow. And as you overfeed it, it becomes heavier and heavier. It also requires more and more feeding to satisfy it, so your burden becomes greater and greater.

In my case the monkey image extends to a famous psychology eexperiment called the "executive monkey." In this experiment a psychologist strapped two monkeys in place and gave them a series of electrical shocks. One monkey, the "executive," was provided a switch that stopped the shock. Each time the psychologist delivered a shock, the monkey would turn it off. Eventually the executive monkey developed ulcers; the other did not. In Sarah's and my case, *I* am the executive. I find the stuff, I process it. All she does is use a little every now and then. The result? I became an obsessed fiend; she did not.

"Monkeys is ze craziest people." They don't think beyond the moment. They do wild and unpredictable things. They are totally untrustworthy. They'll steal bananas out of the mouths of little ones and piss on visitors to the zoo.

If you go about twenty-four hours without stuff you enter the House of Mirrors. In this house all you can do is sit around and think about yourself. You see a reflection within a reflection within a reflection. Senses begin to return, smells are overpowering, sounds echo in your head. You become aware of your body: your legs are down there, your arms are out there. As you progress from Stage One through Stage Four, that awareness changes to pain. Junkies talk a lot about the physical discomfort of withdrawal, but in fact that's not the worst of it. The House of Mirrors is primarily a feeling of fear and despair. As you turn ever more into yourself, the feeling of despair becomes overwhelming and the Fear (a terror without object) causes your resolve to evaporate. A junkie will do almost anything to escape it. It's a terrible feeling.

During the House of Mirrors it's very difficult to sleep. You lie there in bed and your muscles begin to tense. As the tension builds you crave a way to release it. Eventually you get this semivoluntary motion where your body twists and your legs kick (it's the symptom that gave rise to the expression "kicking the habit"). You get a momentary release and then it starts building again. If you somehow manage to fall asleep, you're liable to wake up kicking and ejaculating at the same time. It's weird. I call it "doing the jerk." Doctors call it "clonus."

After about five to seven days you enter the House of Blue Lights. The fear and despair have begun to wane; they are replaced by a pervasive fatigue and sense of discontent. When I was in that high school for young geniuses (which flunked me twice) there was this special place on the side of a high cliff called the House of Blue Lights. It wasn't any sort of house; it wasn't even a cave. It was just a place. Nobody could remember who had given it that name or what it meant, but students had been going there for years. I used to sit there, just killing time, waiting until I could get away from that fucking desert. I wanted to go to places like New York and San Francisco, Rome, Athens, Cairo, Guadalajara, Stockholm, Bangkok, Hong Kong. I eventually went to all those places. Some were better than others. Now I'm sitting here on a muddy little farm in western Washington, trying to kick and missing the dry, dusty old red rocks.

The House of Blue Lights is a frustrating feeling. You don't feel good and you don't feel bad. You feel blah and bored, and it goes on and on and on. It becomes difficult to remember why you decided to stop using. You quickly forget the horrors of the House of Mirrors and start trying (often successfully) to convince yourself that one more hit wouldn't hurt. All you want to do is sit and let time pass. Everything seems grey. If you have to do something, anything, the effort involved seems monumental, impossible. You don't talk much because, try as you may, you can't think of anything to say. I tend to sit in one spot and stare at (not through) the window.

★

Goddamn, motherfucking, shit, piss, fuck! I feel awful! I can't stand this; I can't stand it. I'm going to a hospital somewhere, take gradually reducing doses of methadone. Have nice, clean sheets, fresh daily. Sit in on some group therapy and stuff. Weep and whine to a nice shrink. I can't do this! Betty Ford got to go to a hospital. Johnny Cash got to go to a hospital. When David Kennedy was kicking he got to go to a place that cost twenty grand a month. Me? I go once a week to see a counselor at the local mental health center, where an aging hippie keeps telling me I've got a "sick system." Now what the fuck does that mean?

"It means you're not communicating with the significant people in your life," he says. "You've lost the ability to get your needs met."

"I have?" I ask.

"That's right," he says. "Besides drugs, what do you do for Eric?" He's always trying to get me to refer to myself in the third person. "What really makes Eric happy?"

"When I'm loaded most everything makes me happy," I say. "And when I'm straight, well . . . I don't know. I haven't been really straight for a while."

"You see? You see what I mean? You've got a sick system."

Ted Schimmle has been a drug abuse counselor for a long time. I think he genuinely thinks he's said something when he makes these pronouncements. Maybe he has something specific in mind when he uses words like "communication" or "system," but more likely he's simply rattling off canned statements that he developed years ago, hoping his client responds with something revealing. I know the trick. I've used it myself. I've been a psychotherapist as long as Ted. And that's another difficulty in our relationship. Ted admits he's never treated a professional colleague before, and seeing me kind of gives him the willies. We worked at the same agency three years ago, and my more diversified experience in the field (and my advanced academic degree) have always made him feel a little inadequate to the task of treating me. Myself, I don't give a shit. A dope fiend's a dope fiend—no matter how many diplomas he has hanging on his wall.

"I don't know that my system is so sick, Ted," I say. "I think my problem is that I take too much dope. If I didn't take dope I think my problems would be manageable—you know, just the normal vicissitudes of life."

"Man," says Ted. "You and your three-dollar words. I think you run the risk of intellectualizing your problems."

"I'm not intellectualizing," I say. "I just used a big word."

"Well, okay," Ted says. "I've told you before that I worry you could run intellectual circles around me. I want to be a sounding board for you, someone you can be honest with, let your hair down with. As a therapist, that's all I can really offer. I hope you weren't expecting any more." Ted worries constantly that he can't provide me with what I need. And who knows, maybe he can't. He admits he has a drinking problem, also a weight problem. He's always in trouble for not keeping up on his charting or getting his Title XIX forms in. Sometimes he comes right out and says that his life is in just as much disarray as mine.

"You're not a real junkie," he often insists. "You hold down a good job; you maintain a stable family life. I would consider most of my clients successfully treated if they were in the position you're in."

"I'm a real junkie, Ted," I always say. "I've been using narcotics in one form or another for most of the past nineteen years. That's a junkie."

"No," says Ted. "That's just an example of your low self-esteem. What you need to do is accentuate the positive. Then your recovery can progress."

If Ted Schimmle could see me now, he might be convinced. I tell him I get like this, but I don't think he believes me. Like Sarah, he thinks I exaggerate my drug problem. He thinks I do it because I have a dysthymic disorder, a type of depression. Sarah thinks I do it because, along with all my good qualities, I am, on occasion, a self-pitying asshole who wants people to feel sorry for me so I won't have to do things that are necessary to get out of my *ennui*. *I* think I am the way I am because narcotics cause anybody and everybody to be like this after enough years of regular use. It's as simple as that. Of course it's also true that my self-esteem could stand some improvement, and I must admit that I can see a willingness in myself to accept any sympathy that somebody might feel like tossing my way. Is that different from straight people?

★

Sarah's up. She's doing her twenty-minute aerobics workout with the television. I can't really blame her for being impatient with a man suffering from a self-inflicted problem. I must remind her of her father.

Sarah Detzer was born Sarah Liebling the same year as me, but on the other end of the country in New York City. We married when I had just turned twenty. We came together, two wounded, confused individuals, and remained together against all odds these sixteen years. Sarah was initially attracted to me because of my good drug connections, which she saw as romantic. I found her dark eyes and Semitic features breathtakingly beautiful, and besides, she was an easy lay. All our friends, relatives, and clergymen tried valiantly to talk us out of marriage. The rabbi who performed the ceremony insisted on meeting with us not once but three different times. He called our plans "immature." He finally capitulated when I agreed to convert, though somehow I never got around to doing it.

Sarah's earliest memory is from the age of six. Her mother had shaken her awake at three in the morning saying only, "Your father's sick; we've got to take him to the hospital." Little Sarah sat in the back seat of the cab between her mother and father. Jacob Liebling stared straight ahead, his hands folded tightly in his lap. Breathy, animal sounds puffed from his pursed lips as white spittle collected in the corners of his mouth. Sarah knew he was praying, though even in her six-year-old mind she knew there was a big difference between the way her father prayed and the way the rabbi prayed. "Stop it, Jake," said her mother, Rosalind. "Think of the child, for God's sake." But Jacob kept up his babble, oblivious of the others in the car. He was floridly psychotic.

As a small child Sarah made every effort to love and admire her father, to be a Daddy's girl. She would place her little wicker chair in front of the doorway and wait for Jacob to return home from work each night. At dinner she would laugh uproariously at his made-up words and funny stories. But as the trips to the hospital continued and Sarah found out that, often as not, her father was not there for her when she needed him, the little girl's love turned to a teenager's revulsion. She no longer felt sympathy for her father's endogenous depression, his "illness." To Sarah, he became an excruciating embarrassment. At the age of fifteen, in a fit of loathing, she dubbed him "hideo bitch lips" and thereafter refused to ride along in the cab to the hospital. She spent more and more time away from home and developed a lifelong antipathy toward people who are unable to cope with their emotional problems. She also carries with her, to this day, a secret terror that she might someday be afflicted with the same manic depressive illness that crippled him.

*

"Poor Eric. You really do feel crummy, don't you?" Sarah said just now. "Would you like me to make you some soup or something? You should probably eat."

"No, really," I said. "I wouldn't be able to hold it down." I probably would feel better with food in me, but I know it wouldn't stay there. There's only one thing my body wants right now. Ah, God in heaven, this is terrible. This is the most terrible feeling in the world. And it's only beginning.

"Well I'm going to take Rose and Adam for a picnic," Sarah said. "You want to come with us?"

"I can't, Sarah," I said. "I just can't. I haven't got the strength." I can't believe how whiny I sounded, but I really didn't have the strength.

"Well don't just mope around the house all day, bubaleh," Sarah said. "You'll drive yourself nuts and you'll drive me nuts too. Try to do something; keep yourself busy." I love Sarah. I know how hard it is for her to be understanding and kind about this. I also know that she was hoping I would be of more help around the house on my long weekend off from work. I do love her.

But right now, I need to be alone.

As I sit in my chair, waves of terror wash and break over me. I grip the armrests and tremble. Sweat soaks my shirt. Sweet Jesus, I'd almost rather die. How can I be so sure this will pass? How do I know I won't feel this way from now on? Jesus Christ.

Sarah washed the kitchen floor before she left. The smell of ammonia is still sharp in the air. Through all the years, even the bad ones, Sarah's always been compulsive about a clean kitchen floor. Even when we lived like animals in San Francisco, lo those many years ago, she always kept the kitchen floor clean. For so long after we left, the smell of ammonia always reminded me of San Francisco in the sixties.

San Francisco. Whenever I'm kicking I think of those years: 1968 to 1971. I had decided I wanted to be a real, honest-to-God junkie—play the part to the hilt. The smell of ammonia brings to mind a picture of a frightened, emaciated dreamer. I'm wearing a leather coat and have holes in my shoes. We live in a North Beach apartment that has no furniture other than a bed. We have become creatures of the night: inhabitants of the back alleys and twenty-four-hour cafeterias of the Tenderloin District, the Fillmore, Market Street.

Fast Joey is staying with us and he can score for twenty-two dollars.

My own brother makes twice that much for one hour of straight work and I can't think of a single way to get the money. I run down my various scams. Safeway is on to me: two hundred dollars worth of bad checks before they finally stopped cashing them. I could probably make the Mayfair Market for ten dollars, but they're starting to get wise. I look around the apartment: nothing left to hock. I'm getting desperate. How could I possibly have to suffer like this for lack of twenty-two dollars? Sarah is sleeping. Fast Joey hits four reds and falls asleep. It's 11:00 P.M. Nobody left to borrow from. No telephone. I hit the street.

"Help me out, man, I'm sick," I say to Skinny Jimmy. "I'll owe you one, man. I mean it."

"Fuck you," says Jimmy. "You already owe me. Besides, I'm sick too."

"Jimmy, please, for God's sake. I'm sick, man; I'm sick."

"Fuck yourself," Jimmy says. There's nothing more to say.

Midnight. One A.M. I'm wandering through a parking lot. I see a car with a window open. Inside is a huge camera case. My mind drifts back to childhood, when I could never so much as steal a pack of gum. But I feel no remorse as I open the door of the car, grab the camera, and run. Back in the kitchen I open the case—at least a couple thousand dollars worth of equipment. I fall asleep at the kitchen table.

Morning brings the sickness on—unendurable. My skin is raw, like a thousand roaches crawling underneath. Give the camera to Fast Joey. Tell him to trade it for all the heroin he can. I'm too sick to go along. I lie on the bed and wait.

One hour . . . two, three, four, five, six. Joey is gone. I've been burned.

Furious, I grab my checkbook and head for Mayfair. Cash one ten-dollar check at the check stand, another ten-dollar check in the liquor department. I pray that just this once the clerk won't look at the bad check list. I take the twenty. On the way to Johnny's I see a watch in an unlocked car. I grab it and run. Johnny is nodding when I come in. A quick phone call. Johnny goes down the street, meets Sonny, and brings back the dope. I open the bag and give him his third. I go home and fix. No more high anymore. Just manage to get well. But that's something.

Morning. Surprisingly early considering the lateness of the previous evening. Morning comes creeping in through curtainless windows. The still air of the bedroom is cool and somehow hostile. Sarah is sleeping beside me, looking like a broken doll. She twitches slightly as I drag my aching body out of bed. "Where are you going?" she asks. A curious question. Where am I always going? "Out," I say. That's all that needs to be said. I pull on my pants and shoes, feel in my pocket for my checkbook. How long has it been since I had any money in the bank? Who cares? I'll try to cash one more, just one more.

"Morning, Helen," I beam to the cashier at the corner store. "Could you cash a twenty-five dollar check again? I hate to ride all the way over to the bank. Oh, by the way, put that last check through again. Bank error, ha . . . ha . . . ha. Thanks."

The sickness is on me now. My neck and chest are burning. I can barely move my right foot to put it in front of my left. My nose is running down my face, but I don't have the energy to sniffle. So far the day is going okay; the money is in my pocket. Now please God, let Johnny have some stuff. Please don't make me wait.

I swoon a little on the second flight of stairs in Johnny's hotel. Leaning against the door, I tap my fingernails lightly on the wood. Don't knock loud. You scare everybody in the room if you knock loud.

"Who?" The voice sounds weak and irritable. Damn, he's sick too. Sonny's probably got his phone off the hook, so Johnny isn't able to score. "It's me, partner." I hear the sounds of four different locks being unhooked. The door opens slightly. "Come on."

Johnny's face has the Fear all over it. He is so shrunken and cadaverous he is pathetic. His black skin seems to be turning gray. Thirty years a junkie and he can't make a score. There are two other people in the room, both hookers. Everybody has money, but Sonny won't answer the phone. Noses running, stomachs rumbling, eyes watering, we pool our money to come up with enough cab fare to send Johnny to the Fillmore District. Dope is cheaper there than in North Beach. Johnny puts on a ridiculous hat and leaves. It's 9:00 A.M.

We sit down on the bed to wait. Never quicker than an hour and a half; sometimes it takes all day. You never know and that makes the waiting harder. Sitting, waiting, smoking cigarettes; nobody talks. We look blankly at each other, knowing that nobody can do anything for anybody. All we can do is wait for Johnny. One hour, two hours, three hours.

"He's taking a long time," says Brenda. We look at her. "Jesus, I'm sick."

"It takes as long as it takes," says Gina. We nod agreement.

Finally we hear fingernails lightly brushing the door: *the knock.* I fly to my feet in a superhuman effort. One, two, three, four locks. Open the door. Johnny is gasping for breath and seems on the verge of a heart attack, but I don't feel much concern for my friend's failing health. My only concern is that his cheeks are bulging a little. He has four balloons of stuff in there. I drag him in the door. There will be plenty of time for concern after I have fixed. He gives me two bags.

I open one and pour it in the spoon. Cook. Draw up. Tie off and start the endless search for a vein. The others sigh with envy as I hit blood in the mainline. They have long since worn out their arms. The girls fix in their hands or their necks. Johnny fixes in his leg.

I watch as an air bubble comes up the dropper's neck, followed by the precious blood, which will carry life and strength to my body. I squeeze the dropper faster than I should—burn out your veins quicker that way. The brown liquid empties into my vein. Nothing. I don't feel a thing; I've been burned. Nothing . . . wait.

I feel a soothing warmth start to crawl up my spine. My nasal cavities open. The pain in my legs and arms melts like butter in a hot frying pan. I look around the seedy dope fiend hotel room. I see Johnny's withered face deadly intense, trying to hit that leg vein just one more time. Affection for this kindly old man wells up in my chest. Warm satisfaction has spread over my body. I feel good. I stick the second balloon in my mouth and start for home. The eight-block walk from Broadway back to Grant is now pleasant and I smile at all the passersby.

Turn the corner. In the back door. "Eric, is that you?" Sarah asks. "Did you get some dope?"

"Yeah, I did," I say. "Want some?"

"Sure," she says. "I could use some today. How much did you spend?"

"Nothing," I lie. "I found a watch over on Divisadero and traded it to Johnny for half a quarter-tea. We can split it."

In the next apartment lives a biker chick, Ruby: two hundred and fifty pounds of leather, fat, and tattoos. She can go to Dr. Mann. Nathan Mann is a legend in the Bay Area. Unlike other croakers, you don't have to give him a story. Dr. Mann is crazy. Maybe he has brain damage from alcoholism, maybe presenile dementia, but he doesn't seem to care about anything. You lay ten dollars on the desk and he writes three scripts. But you can't just make an appointment with him; somebody he knows has to introduce you.

I want to meet Dr. Mann. Ruby, I know, wants *me.*

"Well, well . . . hello there, pretty boy," says Ruby as she opens her door for me. "Mmm—you sure look pretty." She knows why I'm here. I'd told her I wanted to meet Dr. Mann. She had said to come over and we'd talk about it.

"Can we go see the doctor?" I ask.

"Sure baby," says Ruby. "You feelin' a little sick, huh?" Ruby chuckles to herself as she nudges me down on the bed. "Sure—we can go to the doctor. But there's no hurry. Relax."

I do feel a little sick.

*

Dr. Mann's office is in a seedy part of Oakland. His practice may have been respectable at one time. Now it is littered with papers and covered with dust. It looks more like a Tijuana abortion mill than an American physician's office. Nathan Mann is a dingy old fool. His shoes are run down and his trouser cuffs are frayed. His white lab coat has a cranberry juice stain on the front and the elbows are grimy.

Ruby lays a ten-dollar bill on the table. "I want seconal, desoxyn, and percodan," she says. Dr. Mann nods and writes the scripts. He hands them to Ruby and stuffs the money in his pocket. He looks at me.

"Uh . . . the same, I guess. The same things." I lay ten dollars on the table.

I can strain and shoot the percodan. Twenty of them will get me off. Desoxyn is methamphetamine: a nice little treat for a junkie, though they're difficult to fix. You have to soak them overnight to get the tablets to give up their goodies. Then you have to let most of the water evaporate, which takes another 48 hours. Seconal, "reds," are necessary to get through the speed crash.

"Name?" says Dr. Mann without looking up.

"Detzer," I say. "Eric Detzer . . . D-e-t-z-e-r."

"What kind of name is that? Russian?"

"We're Finnish," I say. "The family comes from the Ukraine, though, so it's related to Russia." But Dr. Mann has stopped listening. He writes my scripts.

"Don't come back for at least a week," Dr. Mann says to Ruby.

"Right," says Ruby and moves toward the door. Dr. Mann continues to sit, staring at the window.

Only a few pharmacies will fill Dr. Mann's prescriptions. Those that will do a volume business in controlled drugs.

Three days after our visit, Dr. Mann is murdered. Somebody had come back in less than a week. When Dr. Mann said no, his patient slit his throat.

I wonder: Did anybody say Kaddish for old Dr. Mann?

And then the day finally comes. The rent money has gone into my arm and we have to leave our North Beach apartment. Gina the Speed Queen is infatuated with Sarah and invites us to live with her in the Mission District. She lets me come along because she knows that at the rate I'm going I'll eliminate myself in a short time and Sarah will be all hers. A pimp named Talley also has his eye on Sarah. At four foot eleven and ninety-five pounds, he figures she could pass for thirteen and make him some good money. He brings a couple of bags over each day and Sarah is as strung out as I am. Other people drift in and out of the apartment: like crabs and leeches in oily tidal pools. There is activity at every hour of the day and night.

Sarah tucks her head into the nape of my neck. "I'm scared, Eric," she says. "What's going to happen to us?" I don't have an answer for her. I don't know what to do. The sound of an explosion reverberates through the place. There is the sound of feet running down the stairs. Donny is dead on the kitchen floor. Mouse has wigged and decided to waste him for being a snitch.

Gina and Red-Headed Gary drag Donny's body out into the alley.

My brother is twelve years older than I. I put in a collect call to him in Los Angeles. "Jesus, Eric," he says. "I've been worried about you. Nobody knew where you were. I wasn't even sure you were still in the Bay Area."

"I got trouble, Steve," I say.

"Stay right where you are, Eric," he says. "I'll be there in two hours. Don't go anywhere. Just stay right there."

"We'll be here," I say. "And, uh . . . you know . . . thanks."

★

It's raining again. Sarah and the kids have gone to bed. I wish I could sleep too, instead of sitting here remembering the San Francisco days. Jesus—that was fourteen years ago. I remember that, as we sat in the airplane next to my big brother, I figured we were leaving drug addiction behind with Johnny and Fast Joey and the rest. Who would have guessed that fourteen years later, after carving out a nice, middle-class life, I would be sitting here in the House of Mirrors again.

"You're not a real junkie," says Ted Schimmle, my counselor.

Well if I'm not, why do I feel so very awful tonight?

2

The House of Blue Lights

The Chinese brought opium poppies to America. I imagine it happened something like this . . .

Chen Yee Rei stopped running and clutched his side, waiting for the pain of overexertion to pass. Leaning against an alder, he stroked the back of his head and grimaced. The Manchu Dynasty in China had fallen in 1911 and all Chinese had cut the long, braided queues they had worn as marks of subservience. Even now, three years later and half a world away in California, the coarse stubble on the back of his neck felt unnatural to him. He glanced around, watching for signs of movement in the moonlight.

He allowed himself only a moment's rest. It would be dawn in three hours and Chen Yee knew it would be disastrous if he were seen coming in at dawn. The rancher he cooked for did not allow him outside the main compound even during the day. At night he was not allowed outside his room. Chen Yee was taking a terrible risk.

When he reached the river Chen Yee gave one last quick look around, then pulled aside a large, dead branch and half-crawled through a wall of brush. Beyond this hidden gate was a patch of cleared ground, twenty feet long by ten feet wide. The wall of brush around it was so thick that it could not be seen, even from across the river. The clearing had been carefully weeded and tilled. Growing in five neat rows were one hundred plants, each approximately four feet tall. It was August. The petals had fallen from the blooms, exposing seed pods the size of walnuts. Chen Yee allowed himself a soft sigh. He sniffed the acrid smell that indicated it was time to begin harvesting the opium.

Drawing a straight razor from his pocket, he began the tedious, exacting task of slashing the pods. This was delicate work. If he cut too deep the opium would run down the inside of the pod and be lost. Chen Yee took a deep breath. He grasped the stem directly below the pod with his left hand. With his right hand he held the razor in a stationary position. Slowly he moved the pod against the blade and, still holding it by the stem, rotated it against the razor, making a cut two inches long. In the moonlight he could see the white latex begin to bleed out of the cut. Over the next twenty-four hours it would turn to a dark brown gum and be ready to collect. Being careful not to brush against the slit pod, Chen Yee slashed another and another: one thousand pods in all.

Like most Chinese immigrants who grew small, secret opium crops, Chen Yee Rei did not use the drug himself. After three or four cuttings, when the plants finally went dry, he would take his harvest into San Francisco and sell it to the proprietors of opium dens. In this way he was able to provide his wife, Mai Mai, with an occasional silk ribbon for her hair, and even put a little something aside for his children.

He found the old men who smoked opium disgustingly old-fashioned.

As dawn approached, Chen Yee slipped out of his hidden garden and made his way in the dark back to the servants' quarters. He climbed silently over the corral fence and slipped past the sleeping dogs in the backyard of the main house. He padded across the damp lawn.

The rifle shot cracked through the dawn just as the first rays of sun appeared in the East. Lights came on in the bunk house, the servants' quarters, the main house. Voices called across the compound.

"What was it, Zeke? Whadja hit? There a coon in the trash heap again?"

"Nah—it was the Chinaman. Caught 'im lookin' in Missy's window. Right up under there while she was dressin'. Got 'im straight on. He won't be peekin' in no windows no more. Got 'im straight on."

"Whadaya mean, Zeke? You shot the Chinaman? Fer Christsakes you trigger-happy son-of-a-bitch! You shot the Chinaman? Jesus!"

Men came running from various directions, pulling on trousers, some without boots. Everybody talked at once and nobody seemed to know quite what to do. In her tiny shack, Mai Mai sat silently and listened to the incomprehensible voices babbling in English. Though she understood not one word of what was being said, she knew well enough what had happened. She lay a hand on her sleeping daughter's head and stared out the window at the dawn.

Summer passed and the fall winds began to blow. Chen Yee's poppy plants dried and the tiny seeds hardened in the pods. Small holes appeared near the crowns of the pods and the wind shook the seeds out like a salt shaker. Some fell in the river and were carried farther down the bank. Others blew out toward the road and into the fields. Some stuck to the soles of men's muddy boots and were carried back into their gardens. Millions of seeds scattered around the western United States as the descendants of Chinese cooks and railroad workers moved to the cities and abandoned their plants. Hardy, prolific, and beautiful to look at, the flowers began to appear around the homes of ordinary people. Seeds were passed from friend to friend.

"Why Norma—these are the prettiest flowers! What are they anyway?"

"Some kinda poppy, Jean. They were here when we bought the house. They make loads of seeds; I'll give you some in the fall. But be careful now. When you pick the flower it oozes this terrible sticky goo that gets all over your fingers."

★

And so the opium poppy made its way to me: seventy years later and more than a thousand miles away. I found them growing in the garden of our Seattle house in 1976.

"Sarah, where did these red poppies come from?" I asked.

"Judy gave them to me," Sarah said. "She got them from the old lady who lives next door to her."

"What kind of poppies are they?" I asked.

"I dunno; maybe they're opium poppies," Sarah said. "Why don't you try harvesting them?"

It took some doing to figure out the technique. I had to use a single-edge Gillette razor blade to keep from cutting my finger, and it was hard to get the cut shallow enough. Collecting the gum was more difficult than might be supposed; a dull paring knife turned out to work best. It took hours and hours, and my back hurt miserably when I was done.

By the time I was finished I found myself with a ball approximately the size of a very large pea. I was then presented with the problem of how to smoke it. First I put it in a hash pipe and held a wooden match to it, but the damn gook wouldn't light. I realized I would need something a good deal hotter than a flame. After much trial and error, I hit upon an ingenious method. I dug out a one-pint canning jar and put it upside down on the kitchen table next to the stove. I placed the ball of gum on top of the jar, then I turned a burner on and lay a butter knife in the flame. I made a four-inch funnel out of a piece of typing paper and held the tip in my mouth with pursed lips. When the knife glowed red I removed it from the fire and touched it to the ball. As the billow of white smoke appeared I sucked through the funnel for all I was worth, capturing most of the mild-tasting smoke in my lungs. I repeated the process frequently, until nothing was left of the ball except a smear of black on the jar that looked and felt like obsidian. I then laid the knife and funnel carefully on the table, walked into the bathroom, and threw up for the next twenty minutes. When there was nothing left inside me, I flushed the toilet and walked out on the porch to sit down with Sarah.

"Well?" asked Sarah.

"It's opium," I said. And indeed it was.

I could feel the old narcotic glow, so familiar even after my years of total abstinence from opium. I felt warm; I felt comfortable; I felt safe. I felt that overriding sense of well-being that only an opiate user knows. And yet despite the fact that I knew I was high, somehow I didn't really believe it. How could the pretty red flowers Judy had gotten from the old lady next door contain the same active ingredient as the slimy half-load I had bought on 125th and Lexington so very long ago? If it was possible to grow opium in Washington, why was nobody besides me doing it?

*

Seattle is, for the most part, a one-industry town; it makes airplanes. It makes airplanes for the entire world. Today, of course, the Airbus company in Europe, subsidized by several governments, is giving Boeing some competition, but still most air travellers around the world ride in planes made in Seattle. It's always been that way. But sometime in the mid-sixties something happened; I never knew what. The bottom dropped out of the airplane business for a while. Not a long while, but long enough to devastate the Seattle economy. Practically overnight thousands of Boeing engineers and assemblers found themselves out of work. Many of these people were middle-aged and had such ridiculously specialized skills that they couldn't find other jobs. I remember seeing one guy being interviewed by the Eyewitness News Team while standing in the unemployment line. When the reporter asked what his profession was, the man responded that he was a "configuration analyst." That knocked me out: a configuration analyst. I guess that meant his job was to look at how things were put together. Jesus—I wonder how many jobs there are for configuration analysts?

The domino effect was instant and catastrophic. The Boeing people couldn't find work so they left Seattle. When they quit spending their large salaries in town, businesses began to go bankrupt and the owners had to move. The employees of the bankrupt businesses had to move to places where there were businesses that would hire them. So many people had to move that in 1968 some wise-ass put up a billboard on Interstate 5 that read, "Would the last person leaving Seattle please turn off the lights." Ha ha ha. Many of the people who moved had to default on their mortgages. They simply packed up their belongings and went, forcing the FHA to repossess thousands of homes. FHA, of course, did not want all these houses, so they began selling them off at ridiculously low prices. The small, crummy ones they simply gave away.

And so it was that Eric and Sarah Detzer, only one year after flying out of the Mission District with needle tracks on their arms, became the owners of a two-story, four-bedroom home on Capitol Hill, for which they paid eight thousand dollars (of brother Steve's money).

It had been a rough year. Brother Steve had deposited us in Phoenix and then went home to L.A. Many phone calls were made between Sarah's family in New York and mine in Arizona. It was 1971. The two sets of parents decided that they needed to do something about "the kids." Sarah and I simply abdicated, knowing we were too fucked up to make good decisions.

She was sent off to the stately, prestigious New York Hospital in White Plains where several staff members still remembered such former patients as Marilyn Monroe and Judy Garland. I didn't see her again for seven months. I was committed to Maricopa County General Hospital in Phoenix, the psychiatric ward. Some silly law which has since been changed required me to be transported from the ER to the ward on a gurney in four-point restraints. Two deputies with empty holsters served my commitment papers.

"Hope you make it, kid," said one crew-cut deputy. He seemed sincere, though I suspect he said this to all newly admitted addicts. They don't put dope fiends on the psych ward in Maricopa County anymore.

I loved the hospital. I took to life on the ward like a duck to water. The food was delicious and the crisp, clean sheets were luxurious. Twice a day I lined up for medications with the others and I never pushed or complained. I was grateful for my cigarette every hour.

"Sit down, Eric," said the nurse who admitted me. "I just want to ask you a few questions; you know, get to know you a little. Are you okay? Are you up for this?"

"I guess so," I said.

"All right—now, do you know where you are?" she asked.

"Phoenix," I said.

"Do you know where in Phoenix, what building this is?" she asked.

"The hospital," I said.

"That's right," she said. "This is Maricopa County Hospital, the psychiatric ward. Now, do you know the date today?"

"It's April something, 1971," I said.

"Close enough," said the nurse. "I think it's the 13th or 14th, but you're close enough. It's Wednesday, anyway. I'm sure enough of that. Next question: Do you know who I am?"

"No," I said. "I've never met you."

"Oh yeah," she said, chuckling. "I guess I forgot to introduce myself. Sorry. But you could read my name tag, couldn't you? I mean, it's written right here," she said, motioning to the small white badge on her lapel. "Can you read?"

"Yes, I can read," I said. "You're Leslie Anderson, RN, right?"

"Brilliant," said Leslie. "I dub you 'oriented to three spheres.' Now let's go on. I gotta ask you some questions which might sound a little silly, but they're important, so let's go through 'em. First, what does the old saying, 'a rolling stone gathers no moss' mean to you? You know—in your own words?"

I thought for a moment. It was an expression I had heard my whole life but never gave much thought to. It took me quite some time to decide on an answer. "Well, I guess it means that if you keep moving you don't acquire things."

"Right," said Leslie Anderson, RN. "Now, what about 'people who live in glass houses shouldn't throw stones'?"

This one was easier. "If you have faults you shouldn't go around finding faults in others," I said. "How am I doing?"

"You're doing fine," said Leslie. "In fact I don't think I'm going to go on. It's pretty obvious your mental status is intact. You understand, we have to give this exam to everybody who comes in. It's hospital policy. But you're not a crazy, you're a junkie. Junkies aren't crazy."

"Tell me, Leslie," I said. "If I'm not crazy, how did I get myself into the position where it cost me two hundred dollars a day just to get out of bed. Why did I keep shoving poison into my arm every day with a sharp piece of steel, knowing it was only going to make me want more later? Why did I sell all my possessions (and all my friends' possessions) to buy more and more and more of this stuff? Why did I do all the things I did?"

"Because you're crazy," Leslie said.

"But I thought you said . . ."

"Yeah, I know what I said," Leslie continued. "But it's true you're crazy. Crazy as hell. But you're not *crazy;* not like most of the people here are crazy. Take your roommate. He's a chronic schizophrenic, now in acute exacerbation. His mother's been dead for four years. Last week he started hearing her voice coming from under the house. He could hear her calling to him. He tried digging a hole to get to her, but it wasn't fast enough so he got in his dad's pickup and started ramming the side of the house, trying to knock it over so she could get out. It took six cops to stop him. They brought him here and now he just sits there in the day room. Only time he moves is to come get his cigarette every hour. Once we tried to tell him that he had to *ask* for it before we'd give it to him."

"What happened?" I asked.

"The nurse who told him that had to get sixteen stitches in her scalp where he hit her with an ashtray."

"This is my roommate?" I asked.

"Yeah, and he's perfectly safe," she said confidently. "Just don't never mess with his cigarettes. But, anyway, those guys are *crazy.*"

"So what am *I* doing in this nut-house?" I asked, fearful and somewhat annoyed.

"You need to be in the nut-house a while," she smiled. "If you were out there you'd be selling your last pint of blood for a little taste of stuff; that is, if they'd take it from your funky old arm. No—you stay with us a while. Kick back and relax. Drink your methadone and fatten up a little on our shitty food. It may not be much of a place, but it's the only chance you got, homeboy. You walk out that door and you're another dead junkie inside of two years."

"Come on," I said. "I'm not that bad off. Now that I'm away from San Francisco I'll be okay."

"Listen to me, honey," Leslie said, suddenly soft and compassionate. "My baby brother was a junkie. He always said 'I can handle it okay, don't worry 'bout me.' When they brought him in on his last OD he was dead before I could get down to the ER. Everybody thinks they can handle it, and maybe there are some people out there who can take a hit now and then, just on the weekend. But he wasn't one of them—and neither are you. You've been hooked now, and now that you've been hooked you'll never be one of them. I got a saying: Once you been pickled you can never go back to being a cucumber. You kick it, kick it now, and don't you never go messin' with that shit again."

*

Ahhhhh. I wish old Leslie Anderson, RN, was right here now. Back then she was, what? About forty? That would put her in her mid-fifties now. I'd love to have her strong arm around my shoulder and hear the words, "Don't you never go messin' with that shit again" in my ear. She'd understand. She wouldn't laugh at me and say, "Whadaya mean, poppies; you can't get hooked on poppies." She'd know that addiction is addiction, whether it's killing your body or killing only your soul.

Monday is breaking cold and wet over the Cascades. How can I possibly go to work today? It's nearly 7:30. I haven't even shaved yet. I was stupid to think that I could kick over the weekend; it isn't enough time. I think I feel worse today than I did on Saturday. So many times I've gone in, closed my door, and hidden in my office all day, just counting the hours till I could go home. Today I don't think I can even do that. I don't have the energy even to get dressed.

There! Just called in sick for the umpteenth time. That gives me one more day. But what do I do tomorrow, and tomorrow and tomorrow? There is an electric burn pulsing through my bone marrow. The unbearable fatigue consumes me. I know I have to get off this stuff, but now just isn't the time. I can't do it now. Another time—I'll do it another time. Over Thanksgiving—yeah, that's it. I'll do it over Thanksgiving. That's a four-day holiday. That'll give me enough time. I know a place in Seattle, a late-blooming garden, where I can get some stuff; that's only fifty miles. I'll be down there and back to work by noon.

Whew—I feel better already.

★

A peregrine falcon is different from other animals when she feeds. She isn't just hungry; she's obsessed. You can see her fixed stare as she watches for her prey: unblinking, hardly moving. Her favorite is duck. She perches in a tree beyond the river and waits. When she selects her victim (God knows how) from among the flock, her lower mandible moves imperceptibly as she appears to salivate, her eyes glassy. With a quick, silent lurch she leaps into the sky as the duck paddles around, oblivious. Suddenly, a hundred feet up, she stops. She rockets straight down, flapping to pick up speed. She hits the poor, dumb mallard at nearly two hundred miles an hour, knocking it senseless. The other ducks bolt in terror. She doesn't kill with her feet as a red-tailed hawk does; the falcon is far too delicate. If the tremendous impact hasn't killed the duck (and often it hasn't) the falcon carries it to the shore alive. She stands on its back and looks around for trouble, mantling it with her wings. When she's satisfied there's nothing around to steal her prey, she turns her attention to eating. She has a notched bill for quick, easy killing, but for some perverse reason she doesn't always use it. She might simply start ripping strips of flesh from the back of a completely conscious animal.

Falcons, like other predators, have to kill to eat. They have no choice. Who's going to get up at a Greenpeace meeting and say that peregrines ought to be ashamed of themselves for depleting the duck population? Nobody. But why do they do it so . . . passionately? Why do they seem to need, not just the meat but also the kill? Why will they team up with some Arab falconer, even though they are genetically incapable of anything like affection or loyalty, just so they'll have the opportunity to kill more than they can eat? A falcon prevented from killing will soon sicken and die.

A great horned owl is different: different from a peregrine and different from the stereotype. Walt Disney tried to convince us that owls are wise and gentle beings. Bullshit. Owls aren't very smart; in fact, as birds go they're kind of dumb. But what they lack in intelligence they make up in ferocity. The huge, thick talons of a great horned owl can crush and stab the life out of a small dog. The owls' blind indifference to taste and total absence of sense of smell make them the only animals in nature that prey on skunks. They don't care if their dinner is alive or dead; they eat dead cats off the side of the road. They're built for nocturnal hunting, but if they oversleep they'll hunt in the daytime. Crows and other birds hassle owls while they're perched, but the great horned doesn't give a shit. She just turns her head, throws up her rat's bones, and hoots mindlessly until she gets hungry again.

When *I* hit the air, ready to stoop on my place in Seattle, I can feel a sexual quivering in my chest; my lower jaw sets in a salivating position. I don't give a shit about much of anything. I'm circling for a kill . . . and I want the kill as much as the meat.

★

Dope fiends owe a real debt of gratitude to the Germans. The same people who gave us Adolf Hitler also provided us with methadone. The boys in the white coats over at Bayer Laboratories were sitting around trying to think of a cure for an illness that had just recently been defined and named. It was a terrible disease called "morphinism."

It came out of the American Civil War. The boys in blue and grey had shot each other full of painful holes. The field surgeons had few tools at their disposal other than morphine and their brand new invention: the hypodermic needle. They went around poking it into everyone. Some of the boys lived, some of them died, but as long as the morphine lasted, at least they all shut up. Then came Appomattox and the end of hostilities. Orders came from Washington to shut down the field infirmaries and go home. Ooops . . . the soldiers didn't want to go home. The doctors were incredulous. All the boys wanted to do was lie on their squalid cots and take their medicine.

"Honest, doc, it still hurts."

Enter the dread morphinism. The soldiers were carted off to domiciliaries and the boys at Bayer went to work.

What the Bayer scientists came up with made absolutely no sense at all. They took the morphine molecule and made a smaller version of it (the diacetyl form). They then marketed this drug as a *cure* for morphinism. It was to be the champion, the "heroine," to all the poor, strung-out soldiers. Incredible. Of course all the guys who had morphinism were instantly cured by heroin. As long as they took their medicine they could return to normal lives. It was a miracle.

Most of the old soldiers were dead by the time the Harrison Act came along in 1914. William Jennings Bryan pushed this baby through Congress. For incomprehensible reasons, he wanted the Chinese to stop smoking opium. Nobody else really gave a shit and they figured that if it was important to Bill Bryan, why not? Opiate use was pretty rare then. So they passed the act, really just a tax act, and went on to other things, ignoring the consequences of their action.

Enter junkyism. The price of opiates skyrocketed because they were now illegal, and those who were addicted turned to crime. Drug addiction began to grow.

As the new century progressed the Germans began starting global conflicts at an alarming rate. And each time they started a war they cut themselves off from the Turkish poppy fields, just when they needed lots of morphine for their fallen soldiers. By the middle of World War II they were desperate for a synthetic opiate, one that could be concocted in a test tube. Lots of them appeared in the Fatherland, but the best came out of Mallinckrodt Laboratories. It was cheap, easy to make, effective, and it lasted fully twice as long as morphine in killing pain.

"Mein Gott, Fritz; dis iss dynamite shit, ve must name it after der Fuhrer!" Thus Mallinckrodt Laboratories dubbed methadone hydrochloride "dolophine," after Adolf Hitler.

But the Nazis lost the war and people pretty much forgot about dolophine. American physicians began prescribing demerol because they were told it was a nonaddictive substitute for morphine. Things went along as might be expected for several years until about 1965. Suddenly the number of heroin addicts in America began growing by leaps and bounds. It had stayed at about 50,000 for years and years, but between 1965 and 1970 it leapt to 200,000 (200,001 counting me). Middle-class Americans, who had been lied to about the dangers of marijuana and LSD, figured they were equally safe with heroin. The nation panicked, but the medical profession was unable to stem the tide. Their best efforts only seemed to make the problem worse.

Enter Drs. Nyswander and Dole: a pair of New York lunatics (husband and wife) who resurrected the Fuhrer's namesake. They discovered that if they gave junkies enough methadone (dolophine), they stopped taking heroin. Brilliant. They'd line 'em up at their clinic and pump 150 to 200 milligrams apiece into them—roughly enough to kill the entire French Foreign Legion. When these junkies tried shooting a little of the six percent street dope into their opiate-saturated bodies, nothing would happen.

"Like a fart in a windstorm," said Alley Boy, and threw away his bent spike.

Nyswander and Dole heralded their treatment as a "cure" for narcotic addiction, as moronic medical history repeated itself. When methadone inevitably turned up for sale on 125th and Lexington, Drs. Nyswander and Dole quietly retired to New England or something, "so we can spend more time with the grandchildren."

So the score was: opiates, three; medicos, zero. And the search goes on. Now the docs have finally found something that really does not cause addiction: a family of drugs called the nonsteroidal anti-inflammatories. It's true you can't get addicted to this stuff, but unfortunately it doesn't kill pain worth a damn either. Besides, one of them, zomax, has an unfortunate tendency to cause death in certain patients.

Me? I leave it to them to keep beating their heads against the wall. I have little use for their silly "medicines." Give me good old, organic poppy pods, picked right from the plant, blended up into a mash, and strained through a screen like a tea. My technique for making the tea has stayed about the same for years. I fill the blender with pods, add about two cups of boiling water, and puree it for a minute. This leaves a mash that looks like green applesauce. I then strain out the vegetable matter. You need the right kind of strainer. A colander is no good because the holes are too big; a regular tea strainer is no good because it is too fine and the mash clogs it. The best thing is a strainer made with the type of screen used for windows. I hold the strainer over a saucepan and pour the mash in. Then I squeeze all the tea through by mashing it with the bottom of a one-pint canning jar. You pour the tea into a cup and drink. That's it. The stuff doesn't even taste bad.

Within half an hour my nose itches every bit as much as Johnny's or Red-Headed Gary's, and I still have enough money left over to take Adam and Rose to visit their grandparents in New York.

★

Shit. Why do I do that? I was loaded for two days, and now I'm back in the same chair feeling the same things. I don't get it. I hang on for forty-eight hours, maybe seventy-two, digging in my claws, holding on through withdrawal; then *wham,* all of a sudden my will dissolves and I'm gone, saying I'll kick over Thanksgiving. It's especially bad this time of year: fall. All of *my* plants are used up and I have to roam the countryside looking in other people's yards for the descendants of old Chen Yee's secret garden.

After nearly ten years of fussing with opium poppies I can spot them at an unbelievable distance. I've been known to catch a glimpse of pods at a hundred yards away, while driving sixty miles per hour on the freeway. There are, of course, other plants that look similar, but it's rare for me to make a mistake. Opium plants have foliage that is slightly bluish green. They are usually seen in clumps. The little plants appear in April or May and the blooms open in midsummer. I've seen flowers as early as June 20th and as late as November 2nd, but most of them bloom in mid-July. The flowers have been bred to drop their petals (which are red, purple, mauve, pink, or white) as soon as possible: usually after three or four days. Inside the bloom is the magic seed pod.

Actually there is opium all through the plant, but the concentration is much greater in the pod than elsewhere. The pods themselves are green and, at first, quite soft. As they mature they get bigger, harder, and develop ridges running top to bottom so they end up looking like little green pumpkins with crowns on them. As the maturation process continues, the pods develop a whitish blush as if they had been dusted with baby powder. They have an acrid smell and small black dots may appear on the pod's surface where opium has managed to ooze through the tiny holes in the pods. This is the point at which growers slit the pods and bleed out the opium.

By September or October the stalks and pods have usually dried. Inside the pods are a couple thousand tiny seeds. Some subspecies have blue seeds (used for baking) and some have red seeds (used for poppyseed oil, highly prized by painters because it thoroughly cleans oil-based paint from brushes). The dried pods are often used in dried flower arrangements and sold in florist shops. Drying doesn't affect the opium. It is still there, still water soluble. The pods vary in size from smaller than a marble to bigger than an egg. Most of them, though, are about as big as a walnut.

I usually wait until after dark to make my poppy runs so I'm not seen. It's crazy. Sometimes I wonder what would happen if a cop ever stopped me.

"Awright fella, get outa the car and keep your hands where I can see 'em."

"What seems to be the problem, officer?"

"I saw you take something out of that yard back there. Whadaya got in the car?"

"Nothing, officer. I didn't take anything. I was just . . . you know . . . relieving myself."

"What's that in the back seat? Looks like some kinda plant. You got some pot there, buddy? Huh? Let's have a look."

"Why sure. Go ahead and look. It's not pot. It's just some old, dead flowers."

"What kinda flowers, huh? Lemme have a look. Hey . . . looks like poppies. Those opium poppies, buddy?"

"Ho, ho, ho . . . that's good. Opium poppies . . . ha, ha, ha. No—they're just regular old northwestern poppies. Opium poppies wouldn't grow here, I don't think. They're from Turkey or Iran or something."

"What're you doing with those poppies, huh?"

"Doing? Oh . . . nothing . . . they just happened to be in the car."

"Just happened to be . . ."

". . . right. I guess I forgot to dump them out when I was at the dump."

"Well why don't you just dump 'em right now, huh? You savin' 'em for something?"

"No, no, no . . . but I, well, I wouldn't want to make a mess here."

"It's pretty late for dumpin' trash, buddy. And I don't see no dump road here."

"Yeah . . . well . . ."

"You're gettin' some kinda *dope* outa them, aren't you?"

"Dope?"

"What are you doin' with those plants!?!!"

"Nothing!"

"What!!!"

"All right, all right!!! I drive around at night and steal them from old ladies' gardens! Then I make a tea out of them and I drink it to get high!"

"But . . . they're all moldy . . . look, there's an earwig in that one."

"I know."

"Listen, son, maybe you oughta just head home. You look kinda tired."

"Sure."

One of these days other dopers will discover poppy tea. Homegrown opium will be common. There will be lots of hop-heads like me, ranging over the countryside at night, desperately trying to extend the season by one more day. The old ladies' yards will be picked so clean that the poppies will stop coming up. Then I won't seem so ridiculous; I won't be such a freak. But for now . . . it's back to the House of Blue Lights for me.

3

The Cowboy

There's a certain loneliness that can only be evoked by the sound of foghorns cutting through an early morning mist in a big city. Empty warehouses are visible in the half-light; no people are around yet. The call of gulls pierces the diesel smell that lingers from the many years of loading and unloading cargo. Oily water laps the barnacle-covered pilings, and mangy, unwanted dogs roll in the smelly, bloated carcasses of polluted fish. Pop cans, piled kelp, and bits of gooey tar cover the sand. It is not so much loathsome as it is unutterably sad. It gives you the feeling that you're all alone in the world, and the world is not a nice place.

I drove past the waterfront on the way to my place in Seattle and, like the San Francisco waterfront so many years ago, it brought on that melancholy which makes me begin to lose hope. When I feel like this I begin to miss my father, dead now these past twelve years. The raid on the garden went without a hitch and as I drove the fifty miles back to Skagit County, waiting for the opium to hit me, I thought about him and how much I would like to share a few things with him right now.

Old Bud Detzer had two very rare qualities: He never spoke unless he had something to say, and he never judged anybody. If he was here with me now we wouldn't discuss a thing. I'd tell him the problem and he'd agree, "Yep, you've got some real trouble." Then he'd pour us a couple of big mugs of black coffee and we'd sit on the porch and watch the sky—together. My mother would be full of cheerful advice on how to change my circumstances, and then would start pushing on me to "do something." But not Bud. After an hour or two of silence on the porch I'd say, "What should I do, Dad?" And he'd look at me with those soft hazel eyes and say, "Don't let yourself have regrets; whatever has happened has happened. Now do what you need to do." Ah, Dad. Such unwavering confidence in your black sheep, your one bad one out of four.

Bud was born just as the century changed. His family's little one-room shack in the wilds of western Colorado was a seven-day stagecoach trip to the nearest electricity. His mother, a proper lady in impossible surroundings, rode horseback every day to Miss Blood's Finishing School where she taught elocution. At that time my grandfather couldn't work. He was in high, dry Colorado trying to win a battle against tuberculosis which was, at the time, a killer. He puttered around the house. Little Bud, left alone during his early years, developed a much better ability to relate to animals than to people, a condition that would continue the rest of his life. "People are no damn good," I often heard him say, though I know he didn't really feel that way. He always liked the boys down at the gas station and he always liked my wife Sarah. He never knew my children.

Bud's aunt had married a maniacal wheeler-dealer named (believe it or not) P. T., who talked my grandfather into moving to a little town outside of Los Angeles. P. T. assured him it was "the place of the future—it'll make us all rich." It seemed pretty unlikely, but Bud's father Gus was just about over TB, and his mother Dolly had had it up to here with Colorado. So they set out, first by stagecoach, then by train, to California and the sleepy little town of Hollywood. P. T. quickly became impatient, of course, and leaving Gus to watch his real estate holdings, headed out into the desert and began buying absolutely worthless land. "The place of the future!" insisted P. T., who went about trying to get water to it. Unfortunately, P. T. himself didn't live long enough to see what Palm Springs would eventually become.

Gus and Dolly liked the bucolic life in Hollywood fine, so they settled there and Bud went to school. For a country boy whose early education had been neglected, Bud did surprisingly well in school. Unlike the majority of high school students in the twenties, Bud went straight on to college. He spent his first two years at Stanford, but the rah-rah fraternity assholes became intolerable so he transferred to Cal Tech, where he took his degree in civil engineering.

But Bud didn't want to be an engineer. He wanted to be a farmer. He had a couple of bucks, his new wife Rachel did too. So they bought a little farm in the Mojave desert and worked it for seven years. Bud lost money every year. Finally Rachel announced that she was going to go to graduate school at UCLA and live in the city. He was welcome to come with her but she was going. Bud sold the farm, packed up his case of half-pints, and headed into thirty-five years of aircraft engineering and life in the suburbs: first in L.A., then later in Phoenix.

I don't think he was a very good engineer; he was never promoted very far. In order to supplement their income, he played the stock market with money inherited from Rachel's parsimonious father. I *know* he wasn't a good wheeler-dealer and he lost most of the money he invested. He wasn't happy. He drank.

When I was thirteen he suddenly took to his bed. He didn't get up again for a year. We were all told he had scarlet fever or something and we left him alone. When he finally emerged many months later, I was told that he was going to take me on a long trip, which scared the shit out of me because I hardly knew this man. He had been forty-three when I was born. Now we were going to visit relatives who were then living in Bangkok. The idea was for Bud and me to spend time together.

It's weird to travel with somebody you hardly know, especially when you're a teenager. To make matters worse, he had decided to have a father-son talk. I realize now that he was at least as uncomfortable as I was.

I had brought along a monster magazine to look at on the plane, and the moment we sat down I immediately buried my nose in it to avoid having to make conversation. Jesus, I made it hard for him.

"So," he said. "What's that you're reading?"

"It's . . . uh . . . , well, it's a magazine about horror movies," I said.

"Do you like horror movies?" he asked, and once again I was struck by how little we knew each other. I loved horror movies; I still do. *Everybody* knew how much I loved them: my family, my friends . . . everybody.

Bud fell silent for a moment. At the time I figured it was because he had lost interest in the subject. I realize now it was because he was desperately trying to think what to say next.

"You like them a lot, huh," he said.

"Yeah, a lot," I said. "I really like horror movies."

"Like Frankenstein and things like that?" he asked.

"Yeah, I like Frankenstein," I said, "and the Wolfman, and the Mummy." I figured this was all a feeble attempt at keeping the conversation going. I didn't know my Dad was leading up to something.

"How about Dracula?" Bud asked. "Do you like Dracula?"

"Are you kidding?" I said. "Dracula's my favorite horror movie of all."

"Is that a fact?" he said, using one of his favorite turns of speech.

"Yeah, no lie," I said, using one of mine.

"Well then, you ought to find this interesting." He took out one of his thin cigarillos, held it in his teeth, and lit it. "Did you know that the Dracula story was based on a real person? An eastern European count named Vlad Tepes?"

"Really?" I said, beginning to take a genuine interest in the conversation.

"That's right," Bud said. "He lived . . . oh, about five hundred years ago. And what's more, we're related to him."

"You're kidding!" I squealed. I was absolutely delighted. "We are? I mean you and me? Our family?"

"Our family," said Bud. "Vlad Tepes's daughter married a Detzer. In fact, the reason the Detzer family moved to Finland was to get away from Tepes. That's why our name doesn't sound Finnish."

"Wow," I said. I was thrilled. "That's incredible. Me, related to Count Dracula." I basked in my new knowledge a moment; then a thought occurred to me. "Hey, if we're related to Dracula, does that mean we turn out to be vampires?" I was getting a huge kick out of this and I felt let down when Bud didn't laugh at my idea. He just stared straight ahead for a long moment, stone faced. When he finally spoke it was in a soft, serious voice.

"It's interesting you should ask that," he said. "My grandfather told me that members of the Detzer family used to seriously worry about that. And their neighbors back in Finland would blame them every time there was a drought or famine. It's the reason they finally came to America: to escape 'the curse,' or really, to escape from the neighbors who thought they were cursed. It was a pretty serious thing back then."

"Well what do you think, Dad," I asked, still trying to get the conversation back on a lighter note, "do you think we carry a curse?" I tried to punctuate my question with a little laugh, but it came out more like a hiccup.

My dad took a long drag on his cigarillo. "Cursed," he mumbled, still not looking at me. "You know, in a way I do sometimes think we carry a kind of curse. I feel like I've been a victim of it most of my life. And now *you're* growing up. I wonder if you're going to have the same struggle."

⋆

The "scarlet fever," of course, was alcohol withdrawal and, though he did finally lick it, he was a broken man afterwards.

His health deteriorated rapidly and by the time he was sixty-five he was already an old man. He retired to the high canyon country of Arizona, much to my mother's chagrin. He liked isolation. As others began building houses nearby, he walked around the house grumbling, "Next time I move I'm going to dig a hole and pull it in after me!" But he was basically content and for the first time in his life began to relax. When I showed up at the age of twenty-two after getting out of the hospital, he took it in remarkable stride. We sat on the porch. We had a cup of coffee. We made a two-hundred-fifty-mile round trip to Phoenix every Friday night to go to Narcotics Anonymous meetings together.

We did this for six months, until Sarah got out of New York Hospital. Then she and I reconciled and went to live in Seattle. We arrived in the Emerald City (at that time called the Queen City) on October 19, 1972. I stayed clean for three years.

Bud was only sixty-nine when abdominal cancer of some sort killed him. He suffered: two long, slow years of gradual deterioration. When he finally went down he was doubled over in pain, his breathing labored and shallow. The sympathetic country doctor gave him a big shot of demerol (a drug known for its tendency to cause respiratory arrest), sat back and waited for the inevitable. As the drug took effect, his weary lungs gave up and he at last lay dead. Did Doc Steinbeck nudge him over the brink with his injection? I like to think so. Bud had been eager to get on with the next stage; without the shot he may have lasted another day, week, month. He didn't want to wait. Doc Steinbeck gave the injection, then asked my mother for a glass of water, which he drank slowly. Half an hour later my mother called me in Seattle.

I had been waiting for the phone call for months, but somehow when it came I was taken completely by surprise. To this day I can hear my mother's soft, relieved voice across the long-distance line from Oak Creek Canyon to Seattle: "Dad just died." God how it echoed in my head: Dad just died . . . Dad just died . . . Dad just died.

It was purely coincidence, of course, that I started chipping around with drugs again right after his death. I'm no Freudian. I know the world doesn't work that way. I would have started again even if he had been alive. But I wonder. If he were here right now, would we have a cup of coffee on the porch? Would it help to hear him say, "You do what you need to do."

He hated funerals and refused to have one, but we did put together a little memorial service where I read, at his request, the prayer of St. Francis of Assisi that describes the feelings of the social worker he had always wanted me to become:

> Lord, make me an instrument of Your peace. Where there is hatred, let me sow love; where there is injury, pardon; where there is doubt, faith; where there is despair, hope; where there is darkness, light; and where there is sadness, joy.
>
> O Divine Master, grant that I may not so much seek to be consoled as to console, to be understood as to understand, to be loved as to love; for it is in giving that we receive, it is in pardoning that we are pardoned, and it is in dying that we are born to eternal life.

Do you suppose Bud thought it was possible for a person to actually *be* like that? Really have that kind of selflessness? Yeah—I think he did. I think he thought that there were lots of people like that. I think he thought old St. Francis himself was like that. And that he, Bud, was a miserable, inadequate son-of-a-bitch because he couldn't measure up to that ludicrous standard. I wonder if he knew that the record shows Francis of Assisi weighed a mighty three hundred pounds and that, despite his reputation as a protector of animals, he probably *ate* as many of the adorable, furry little things as he protected. My guess is that Bud was twice the man Francis of Assisi was—despite all the whiskey he drank and the money he blew.

★

There used to be a musician named Tim Hardin; he was popular when I was in college. He wrote this great song called "A Reason to Believe." He was a good songwriter; Johnny Cash made his "If I Were a Carpenter" into a big hit. He put out an album or two himself. Then one day he was gone, just gone. No more songs, no more albums, no more concerts; he just vanished. I forgot about him. So did everybody else.

Then one day I saw an interview with him in *Rolling Stone* that broke my heart. The picture of him was, as they say, worth a thousand words. He looked fat and insipid. Tim Hardin was on methadone maintenance. He had gotten strung out on heroin with the money he had made from his wonderful songs. He tried to kick; he couldn't. He went into a program; still he couldn't kick. Finally, in desperation, he agreed to methadone. He figured he'd stay on it a while, until he got his "shit together," then he'd detox. Well, last I heard his shit still wasn't together.

It's been a long time since I read the article and I didn't pay very close attention, but I remember he sounded extremely bitter. He kept talking about a comeback. Poor old Tim just didn't realize what methadone would do to him. Few people do. Tim probably knew it would keep him from going on tour. It doesn't take a genius to figure out that if you have to pick up your dose every morning at seven you can't go on the road. What he probably *didn't* know was that methadone would keep him from being able to write songs. When he was an anguished young junkie he had the full range of emotions: love, fear, joy, pain. Methadone eliminates all that. The only thing methadone users feel is pissed off. How many songs can you write about being pissed off?

I envy Tim. I wish I was on methadone maintenance.

Old Bud would say I'm crazy. The dumb cowboy really believed it was better to feel pain than feel nothing. "If you don't hurt sometime," he said, "how do you know you're alive?"

Dumb fucking cowboy—Jesus.

4

A Reason to Believe

My time to get poppies is 3:00 A.M. Night owls have gone to bed and early risers aren't up yet. It's still dark. I get up at 3:00, hit one or two of my places, and am back in bed by 4:00. I sleep another couple of hours; the relaxed, confident sleep of a dope fiend with a stash.

There are all kinds of crazy myths about opium poppies. The biggest myth is that the color of the petals makes a difference. I've heard people argue at length over which color are "the good ones." People also argue about whether it's the four-petal blooms or the cluster blooms that give the good stuff. All nonsense. They come in red, purple, pink, mauve, and sometimes white. They have any number of petals. Some plants are big and prolific (four feet tall with fifty pods), others are small and can have as few as one pod. Some pods are much more potent than others, but this has to do with soil composition, not with the number or color of the petals. The big orange oriental poppies (which are perennials) have no opium whatsoever. Neither do the little orange California poppies or the Shirley poppies.

There are also things people don't know about opium. A friend once told me she got a "passive hit" just walking through a poppy field in Turkey. She thought it was some sort of psychological contact high. The truth is, she got wrecked on opium, like Dorothy Gale when the Wicked Witch of the West threw a poppy field between Munchkin Land and the Emerald City. The air around the plants gets thick with the stuff and enters your bloodstream through your mucous membranes. Opium growers know it's time to harvest when they wake up with a pounding headache and spend the morning throwing up. The guys who do the harvesting and processing get addicted because the amount they absorb through their skin is enough to produce a pretty good-sized Jones. Drug-sniffing dogs are now trained by using an artificial substance that resembles opium, because their trainers found that when they used the real stuff the dogs got strung out. Really nasty shit, opium.

There are a lot of myths about how opium makes you feel, too. Samuel Taylor Coleridge said, "For he on honey dew hath fed / And drunk the milk of paradise." People think it puts you into a dreamy, hallucinatory state—causing visions of Xanadu and nightmares of Life-in-Death. Good old Coleridge: He really ran a line of bullshit. Cocteau was a bullshitter, too. He claimed it took opium to produce *Beauty and the Beast* and said it was like walking through silk.

There's nothing classy or poetic about opium. It has the same effect as morphine or heroin. You get relaxed and energetic at the same time. Problems seem unimportant. You feel sleepy, but if you go to bed you lie awake. You itch all over. You get constipated. You get hungry, particularly for sweets. You get very patient and understanding. You get nice.

An opium high can be described in one word: comfortable. It's weird that people get to where they'll give up their souls for stuff that just makes them comfortable.

As soon as the opium high hits me, when my nose starts to itch and my panic subsides, I immediately lose interest in drugs. I don't want to talk about them; I don't want to think about them. I won't even make plans for how to get my ration for the next day. As soon as I'm high I turn my attention elsewhere, and for the next twelve to twenty-four hours I pretend I'm a normal person. I don't tell anybody I'm high. In a sense, I guess I'm not high. When I'm in the Monkey House, being baked is my normal state. Even my kids don't know whether I'm high or not on a given day. All they're aware of is that during June, July, August, and September I'm consistently one hell of a lot more fun than the rest of the year.

★

Sarah and I dragged the beat-up old dinghy onto the shore of the island. Near the bay the Skagit River breaks up into dozens of little waterways, leaving large islands. The Game Department owns the land, which they open for duck hunting six weeks a year. During the other forty-six weeks, the two thousand acres of tidelands are all ours: Sarah's, Adam's, Rose's, and mine.

"Let's make sure we've got everything," I said. "Backpack, sleeping bags, axe . . . where are the dogs?"

"Here they come," said Adam, and Bell, an Australian shepherd mix, and Jesse, a husky mix, bounded out of the river and shook water all over us.

"Yuck!" screamed Rose. "Got me all wet."

"Let's sit on the beach a while," said Sarah. "I'm not quite ready to shlep all that stuff out to the campsite yet. The kids can play in the water."

"Yay!!!" yelled Adam.

"I don't wanna play in the water," said Rose. "Too cold. I want you to tell me a story."

"No . . . no stories," I said. "I'm no good at that." What would I tell her . . . about the time I was after poppies and an old lady exploded out the door and chased me out of her garden with a broom?

"Yes, you are," said Rose. "You tell good stories."

"Let's just sit and talk or something," I said.

Rose sat beside me with her thumb plugged in. Sarah stretched out on the other side, her head in my lap. With her left hand she reached up and stroked my back gently. She made a sound almost like a purr. "This is nice," she said.

I was very comfortable. One hundred and twenty-seven thoroughly blended pods had gone into my morning tea. I think I was purring a little myself.

"Are we Jews?" Rose asked. Kids sometimes come right out of the blue with their questions. I thought about it a minute, then decided to go with it. Sure, why not? It would be nice to think of myself as something besides a dope fiend for a few minutes.

"Yeah, I guess so," I said. "We're Jews."

"Well, Amy says Jesus was a Jew and you said we don't believe in Jesus so she must be lying, right?"

For a moment I tensed myself, thinking about telling Rose I don't believe in *anything* but opium. But you can't say that to a kid. "Jesus *was* a Jew," I said tentatively, not at all sure I wanted to get into it.

"Then how come we don't believe in Jesus?" asked Rose. I looked down at Sarah, who gave me a you-got-yourself-into-this-now-you-get-yourself-out smile, but didn't open her eyes. Adam was running around us, spraying sand.

"You dummy," he said. "When Jesus was alive there weren't any Christians. He was the first one."

"What does 'Christian' mean?" asked Rose, not about to drop it.

"It means you believe in Jesus," said Adam.

"Well what does 'Jew' mean?"

"It means you're Jewish," said Adam.

"But what does *that* mean?" Rose persisted. I get into these ridiculous conversations when I'm baked. God knows why. For some reason I decide the kids' spiritual development has been neglected and if I don't provide them with some, they'll end up like me: believing only in chemistry.

Adam turned to me. "Yeah . . . what *does* it mean?" he asked.

"Well," I said, "in the old days there were all different kinds of people who believed in all kinds of gods. Then about four thousand years ago there was this guy named Abraham who struck a deal with a god named Yahweh. Abraham agreed to believe in only Yahweh and in exchange Yahweh agreed to give Abraham's family some good land."

"Abraham was a Jew?" asked Rose.

"No, Abraham was a Hebrew."

"So what does that have to do with Jews?" she asked.

"I'm getting to that," I said. "Abraham and Yahweh made a covenant."

"Does that mean they signed a contract?" asked Adam.

"No, they didn't sign anything. All Yahweh asked was that the men in Abraham's family get circumcised."

"What does that mean?" asked Adam.

"It means that they cut about half an inch off the ends of their winkles."

"They what!?!!" both kids roared in unison.

"You heard me," I said.

"Their *winkles?!!"* All families have their own slang word for the male genital. Penis is too clinical and the established slang words are a little vulgar.

"I know it seems crazy," I said. "But that's what Yahweh wanted and the Hebrews wanted the land.

"Yuck," said Rose.

"Anyway," I said, "Abraham's grandson is the one who finally staked out the land. His name was Jacob, but he was called Israel. He had twelve sons and each of them started a tribe. Then all the tribes except one disappeared. That was the tribe of Judah, so the people in the tribe were called Jews."

"Did they cut off their winkles, too?" asked Rose, giggling uncontrollably.

"They didn't cut them *off*," I said. "Just the tips."

Rose held out two fingers to simulate scissors. "Come here, Adam," she taunted. "Time to cut your winkle."

"Help, help!" squealed Adam. "She's trying to circus-size me!" He took off running with Rose in pursuit.

Sarah finally looked up. "So much for your lecture on theology," she said.

"I just wanted to give them a little of their heritage," I said, "just so they know what they are." I'm sure I sounded very intense.

"Knock off your bible-thumping for a while, will you," Sarah said, "and come give me a kiss." She raised her face to mine and kissed me gently, flicking her tongue against my lips.

Over the last three or four years Sarah has at last begun to age. A grey hair or two has sprouted and the circles around her eyes have begun to appear without provocation. But age agrees with her and she looks better now than she did when she was a wispy, delicate teenager. When we first met I was always afraid she might break. She's much more a woman now and I like it better. I'm glad she didn't get fat.

Adam startled us by wailing, "Wooo wooo wooo! A porno movie!" Rose ran up too, apparently having given up trying to circus-size her brother. "Don't you guys ever get tired of kissing and hugging?" Adam asked.

"Would you rather have us fighting?" I asked.

Adam rolled his eyes. "Kiss all you want," he said. Sarah and I have always fought a lot. It took me a while to get used to it. I grew up in a family that never spoke a cross word, and during our first few years together I frequently thought Sarah and I were on the verge of divorce. But now that I've mastered the New York style of saying what's on your mind, I like it better. So many of our friends had these terribly civil relationships, but they are the ones who ended up divorced. Sarah and I have always kissed and hugged a lot, too.

"Let's get going out to the campsite; I'm hungry," Adam said.

"I don't want to go to the campsite," said Rose. "I'm too hungry. I want to cook here."

Adam said, "Yeah! Let's cook here!"

"It's okay with me," I said. "Sarah?"

"Sure," she said, "but only if I get three kisses from each of you first."

I sent the kids off for firewood and began emptying the backpack. Sarah stretched out with her hands behind her head, gazing at the sky. "Goddamnit," she said. "Why can't it always be like this?"

★

My kids have always called me "Papa." I'm not sure why. I think that, before they were born, I decided I was going to be a different kind of father. When I was a boy a "Dad" was a guy who was gone for work by the time I got up in the morning. We never heard from him during the day; he wouldn't call to say hi, and he wouldn't come home for lunch. He'd return about sundown, collapse in his easy chair (the very one I sit in now), and sigh to my mother, "Uhhh . . . I'm weary." He'd eat his dinner silently while my mother, my sister Katie, and I would blather on about this and that. There wasn't much he could contribute to the conversation anyway. The things he did during the day were boring; at least, I guess they were boring. He never said. His job was to draw pictures of parts of airplanes. He sat at a desk. He hated it. On weekends I was always off somewhere with my friends so I didn't see him. I imagine he puttered around the house. In the evenings he watched some television and read whodunits. I decided I would not be that sort of father; I would not be a "Dad." So I became Papa. It sounded awkward and affected at first, but now sounds just fine. When I overhear Adam talking to his other eight-year-old friends he refers to me as Dad. Kids don't like to seem different. But when we're alone together, or it's just the four of us, I'm always Papa.

And it *is* different for me. Neither of my children will ever say that we met for the first time at age twenty-two. I have known them well since birth. I remember once when Adam was four; I was reading a story to him. My voice got a little gurgly, but I decided to wait until I finished the sentence before clearing my throat. It was a long sentence and Adam heard a bit of gravelly voice before I cleared it.

"Papa," he said, "what's the matter with your voice?" I could tell from his tone that he was genuinely concerned.

"I've just got a frog in my throat," I said absently. I wanted to get on with *Charlotte's Web*. I didn't give any thought to how unusual a situation it would be, taken literally—the way a four-year-old takes things.

Later that day I eavesdropped a little on a conversation between Adam and his cousin Peter. Adam was obviously affecting a rough, gravelly voice. "What's the matter with *your* voice," I asked, knowing he was begging the question.

Adam furrowed his brow as though he were thinking deeply, trying to remember the explanation I had given him earlier. Apparently he could recall that it had to do with a part of the body and with an animal, but his memory was no more specific than that. He thought for a long time; then he took a deep breath, maybe crossed his fingers, and said, "I've got a duck in my heart."

My girl Rose loves to sit on my lap. Like the grandfather she never knew, Rose likes to just sit together not saying much. She likes to stroke my face, twirl her hair, and of course suck her thumb. She is three years younger than Adam. Once, when we had been sitting silently for some time she suddenly pulled her thumb out of her mouth and looked intently at it, a baffled expression on her face. She looked up at me briefly, then returned to studying her thumb. Finally she twisted around in my lap so she was facing me and asked earnestly, "Papa, why do grownups have thumbs?"

Rose has imaginary friends. Her closest friend is Siki, who lives "in California." Sometimes Siki is on vacation and once, right after Sarah's Uncle Jerry died, Siki died too. But unlike Jerry, Siki returned to life within a week. Siki and Rose have a lot in common; many of the things Rose knows, she learned "from Siki." Siki has a friend—an acquaintance really—named Bobo. He is very tall and apparently he is bad, not good like Siki. Bobo causes Siki no end of problems, but Siki always manages to handle Bobo with aplomb. She never lets him get away with his shit.

Once, when Adam had asked an impossible-to-answer question ("Papa, what's God?"), I found myself completely tongue-tied. Rose had no trouble though. She shot back effortlessly, "Adam, God is the *world's* imaginary friend."

Adam is eight, three years older than Rose. Handsome as Adonis and tempestuous as the wrath of God, he can elicit rage as quickly as love from me. He loves stories of intergalactic warriors and cannot decide whether he wants to be a wildlife biologist or a rock 'n' roll singer. His teacher reports that he is given to deep, ponderous thoughts and, even in the second grade, worries himself sick over his school performance. I spend more time trying to get him to forget about schoolwork than I spend trying to get him to finish his homework. His grades are fine if unremarkable. School has knocked a lot of creativity out of him.

I worry about Adam; I worry a great deal. Already I can see in him the seeds of the obsession that eventually tore apart his father, grandfather, and great-grandmother (Bud's mother Dolly, the proper lady of Miss Blood's Finishing School, was a morphine addict in her later years). When he gets it in his head that he wants a candy bar, or wants to go for pizza, or wants to go to a movie, he cannot abide having that desire thwarted. It's not that he throws a temper tantrum; rather, he shows a frenetic frustration, which causes him unbearable anguish. I can foresee a day when drugs and alcohol will replace pizza and candy; when he, like I, will swoop falconlike on the city in search of prey. And when that day comes he will have learned from watching me while he was eight just how Detzer men go about dealing with the chemical bloodlust, the "curse."

A year ago, during my last unsuccessful attempt to kick, I wrote a letter, which I then stashed away in a safe place. My plan is to wait until the day when I know he has passed the point of experimenting with drugs and has begun to have a problem with them. Then I will give him the letter. By that time I will have been drug-free for a while. I know that's true because if I'm not drug-free I will be dead, perhaps by my own hand.

I call it: A letter to my son.

As I write this you have just passed your seventh birthday. You can't read yet and wouldn't understand anyway. I want to tell you some things about me, and maybe when you're older you can learn from my experience. Maybe you'll be fifteen, maybe sixteen. Maybe the time will never come.

In most ways I'm perfectly ordinary. I am thirty-four years old and have been married to your mother for fifteen years. I am a college graduate with a master's degree. I have a steady job in one of the professions and I am good at what I do. I have a nice house with a big garden. Your mother is an accomplished artist and your four- year-old sister is just as happy and healthy as you. I make a reasonable salary. Both cars are paid for.

There is one other thing you should know about me. I am a drug addict.

I have been using drugs for the past eighteen years. I'm trying to stop now and sometimes I think I won't be able to. But as I hold your smile in my mind's eye, I know I must.

How did I get started? I have been asked this question a hundred times. I have asked myself a thousand times. Over the years I have given various answers, none of which was accurate. I didn't start using drugs as a rebellious act. I've never been a rebel. I didn't start in an attempt to medicate against depression; I've never been clinically depressed. I didn't get started in an effort to be cool, nor did I start because I watched my parents pop pills. I had other reasons.

Most of the "experts" in drug abuse say that people start using drugs because of something they call "peer pressure." That means they think that friends encourage friends to use drugs. I don't know, perhaps that's true for some. It was not true for me. When I began using drugs heavily, I had to hide it from my friends. When I graduated from drug abuser to drug addict, I had to seek out new friends. I thoroughly disliked these new people, but in order to get drugs I had to associate with them. Nobody turned me on to dope. I sought it out and pursued it.

I started using drugs at a time in my life when I was searching for something to believe in. I knew the Beatles were wrong when they insisted that "love is all you need." I also suspected the church was wrong when clerics admonished me to trust in God. The American dream of wealth and success had little appeal for me. I smoked my first joint when I was sixteen years old and knew I was on the right track. When, a few months later, I took my first hit of speed, I knew I had found what I was looking for: *I had found something I could believe in.*

I experimented with the psychedelic drugs in high school, but these had the wrong effect on me. I did not want my consciousness expanded. I wanted it constricted. I wanted to eliminate the entire range of emotions except happiness. I did not want my feelings to be at the mercy of external events. I wanted control—total control. I wanted to be able to *buy* my sense of well-being. Amphetamines, and later narcotics, allowed me to do this. People could hurt me, events could surprise me, gods could desert me; but dope was always the same, always good, and predictable as the rising sun. I could believe in it absolutely.

By the time you read this you will have heard, again and again, how it took me eight years to get through college. You may or may not have heard the reason why. It seems impossible to believe now, but during my freshman year I did not realize how dependent I was on drugs. It was the sixties, and all kinds of drugs were available and relatively cheap. I rarely went without. During those brief periods when my sources dried up I would become screamingly unhappy, but assumed this was because I was away from home for the first time. I saw a psychiatrist briefly. He thought owning a car ("getting wheels," he called it) would solve my problem.

Halfway through my sophomore year it finally became clear. I received a notice from the school that I was on academic probation. I realized I had not been to class in weeks. I didn't even know which courses I was signed up for. It was clear to me that I was only interested in drugs. I dropped out of school.

In those days the drug mecca was San Francisco, so it is not so surprising that we moved there. Your mother wanted to go to school at the Art Institute. I wanted to take drugs. I wanted her to take them too, so she did—though unenthusiastically. I had a couple of jobs for a while, but lost both as a result of my obsession. My world became smaller and smaller, until it included only your mother and drugs.

I shot so much speed that I stopped getting high. The comedown, the crash, became increasingly unbearable. In order to take some of the edge off speed, I began shooting heroin. As I became addicted to the heroin, I had to give up speed. I could no longer afford it. When you're a heroin addict you can't afford anything except heroin: rent, electricity, even food. It is assumed that one becomes a criminal.

I didn't make a very good outlaw; I was afraid to rob and steal. I made my money passing bad checks and taking out bogus loans. I had something few junkies have: an honest face. The law caught up with me, of course. We had to leave San Francisco in the middle of the night. Your ever-optimistic Uncle Steve provided the tickets.

As I look back on those days, I marvel at my naïveté and stupidity. Believe it or not, it came as a surprise to me when my little world was blown apart. I thought I could keep a secret.

During the months that followed, I pulled myself together. I got treatment and I stopped using drugs. I finished college and graduate school. I stayed clean. Your birth occurred during this period; three years later your sister was born. But between your birth and hers I made the mistake that so many of us make. I started using narcotics again recreationally. I justified it by using the same rationale that junkies have used since the passage of the Harrison Act in 1914. "It's okay," I said. "I can handle it."

My relapse began slowly: once a month, twice a month, once a week. I continued to work. I was a good father, a good neighbor. I paid my taxes. But even as I was assuring myself that I could handle it – I knew I could not.

You're seven years old now; your sister is four. I am no longer the junior gangster I was in San Francisco. I know how to grow and extract my own opium now so it doesn't even cost much to stay high. A few days ago I tried to explain to you why I don't feel like doing much any more, why I'm tired and irritable most of the time. I tried to explain that it was those pretty flowers that gave me the energy to kick the ball around with you. Without them I can barely get myself out of bed. Your response cut me to the core. "Why don't you take some of the stuff," you said, "and let's play some ball."

I can understand you feeling that way, but it hurts me to think it has come to this. That I'm never happy unless I have drugs in my bloodstream. That opium has become an integral part of my personality. That I am not a whole person without my stuff. You don't like me and I don't like you unless I'm loaded. Can you see, now that you're a teenager, how impossible this situation is?

You will have had many lectures in school about the dangers of drugs. You will be told how they harm your body and cause you to act erratically. These lectures never had much of a deterrent effect on me and you will probably be the same. The truth is, it's possible to stay reasonably healthy and functional while using large quantities of dope. I am living proof of that.

No, the negative effects of drugs are not physical and not social. They are spiritual.

You know that I am not religious. It's been awkward and difficult for me to try telling you about God; more awkward than telling you about sex. I don't know if I believe in God. But I do know that every person has a spirit, and the spirit is vulnerable.

Opiate drugs poison the spirit, rob the user of his soul. My spirit has been so battered and anesthetized that I wonder if maybe it isn't too late for me. Only time will tell. But you're still very young (though I realize that at times you feel as old as time itself), and there is still time for you to stand back and look at what you might be doing.

Despite it all I don't think I'm a terrible person. In many ways I'm a good and decent man. I've accomplished things I'm proud of. My wish is that I could change the normal course of human development, cut across the grain that has been so firmly set for so many thousands of years, and somehow arrange it so that in this one area you could learn from *my* experience and not have to bear this cross yourself. That would make it all worthwhile.

★

I don't worry about Rose, at least not in that way. I could be completely wrong, but I don't see her getting strung out. I do see other things down the road, though. Rose is a toucher. She loves the feel of body against body: kissing, hugging, caressing, even just holding hands. If she is afraid, confused, or sad she deals with it by finding somebody to touch. She and Sarah have daily times when they sit in the easy chair or lie on the bed and just "nushy": our word for affectionate touching. Adam likes a little nushy now and then too, but Rose needs it several times a day. Sarah's a toucher too, and the two of them can spend hours just talking and nushying. About the time Adam is discovering drugs, Rose will be discovering sex. And my guess is that she is going to love sex. But her early experiences with it hold the potential for being painful and confusing.

Not everybody sees sex as an expression of affection. There are those who see it as an expression of dominance. There are even those who see it as a form of violence against women, and teenagers have been known to make poor choices of sex partners.

But maybe I'm wrong about that. Who the hell knows what the kids will end up doing. And God only knows what they think about poppies. They're really too young to understand that eating the potatoes and carrots out of the garden is good, but eating the poppies out of the same garden is bad. I'm not sure I completely understand the difference myself. And they couldn't possibly understand what "high" means. How could they? I've told them how using poppies screws me up, so they echo my own words back to me, but I suspect they don't have a clue *why* they should cause problems. And all my relapses only serve to confuse them more. I'm sure that both kids would be happiest if I just shut up about poppies.

I remember once when I got in from a late-night raid and Adam was already up. He came running out the back door to greet me.

"Papa, papa," he yelled, beaming happily. He had been watching out the window, waiting for me. Sarah had told him that I had gone out for a little "alone time." "Where've you been?" he asked.

"Oh . . . just out for a drive . . . here and there . . . you know." I tried to slip quickly out of the car so he wouldn't see what I had in the back seat: fifty-three poppy plants I had taken from a garden in Sedro-Woolley, a nearby town. I had trouble with the seat belt though, and by the time I freed myself he was hanging on the open window of the driver's side.

"Did you get anything for me? A candy bar?" he asked, still beaming and so glad to see me.

"No . . . uh . . . no stores were open," I said, "but we can go out in a few minutes and get something. C'mon, let's go in the house and see what Mommy's doing." I tried to hustle him away from the car, but it was too late. He had already gotten a good, incriminating look in the back seat.

"You got poppies again!" he wailed angrily. "How come you keep saying you're not going to do poppies anymore and then you keep getting them?!"

"I wish I had an answer for you, son," I said. "I do want to stop, but somehow I just don't seem to be able to. I can't seem to stop myself." I was hoping he'd see it as I did: that I was in the grip of a compulsion too strong to resist. He didn't.

"Damnit bullshit!" he yelled with tears in his eyes. Then he ran into the house to watch TV. He was four years old.

I wanted to run after him, hold him near me, and assure him that, no matter what might happen, I would always be there to take care of him. But I didn't. Instead I let him watch TV and I went down in the basement to process the pods. I knew I could turn his mood around later. I could buy him a toy, just some cheap piece of molded plastic, and he would immediately get happy again and stop thinking about my confusing, mixed message about poppies. Incredibly I am always able to make myself believe that my double-talk, manipulation, and bribery of him will not cause any serious, long-standing problems.

"Besides," I always assure myself, "this is the last time I'm going to get poppies."

*

Thanksgiving has come and gone without me even trying to kick. Soon it will be Christmas. I have been using heavily for nearly three weeks. I had an incredible bit of luck. I was driving around Samish Flats, out where all the raspberry farms are, just killing time. I turned down a little road I'd never noticed before. There were no houses around, just an old, dilapidated barn. Behind the barn were the overgrown remains of a garden, and in the garden, next to the dried-up corn stalks, were several hundred *papaver somniferum* plants.

I called it my "muthaload."

So I've been high for three weeks and there are enough pods left for maybe another week, week and a half. Then what do I do? My habit has quadrupled as a result of this. It's going to be hell to kick a Jones this big. Also, these are probably the last poppies left in the valley. I've already cleaned out most people's yards and any that remain will be starting to rot now that the rains have come. Jesus. And what do I say to Sarah? She thinks I quit a month ago. Just yesterday she was saying how nice it is now that I've got my energy back.

Ah Sarah . . . so many years together, so many things we've faced side by side. The first time I saw her I had the sense that electrical wires were crossing and short-circuiting in my head. There were fizzles and pops throughout my nervous system. She was the most desirable female I had ever seen. The day we met I moved in with her and, except for the time she was in New York Hospital, we have shared the same bed ever since.

I've always felt there was something magical about her, that there was a power and a passion in her that has been growing and refining over thousands of years. Sometimes I think she must be the daughter of David and inherited her father's violent temper, uncontrollable sensuality, and limitless devotion. She agreed to marry me only because there seemed to be no good reason not to, but during the ceremony she vomited at the rabbi's feet.

She didn't want to get married. She was afraid it would change things between us.

During the early years we had a shared fantasy of being Bonnie and Clyde: rippin' and runnin', playing at being bad guys. We did everything together; we were never apart. I think it took about ten years before she stopped feeling hurt and abandoned every time I went to work. We delayed having children for nine years, being too caught up with each other to need anybody else.

We met when I was in college in Vermont. She had wandered up to New England for no particular reason and stayed with me because she had no particular place to go. After one torturous winter she announced that she was going to San Francisco and it didn't even occur to me to stay behind. We crossed the Bay Bridge in April of 1968.

Neither of us had any idea how to function in the "real world," nor did we know that we didn't know. We only had six hundred dollars between us, so we checked the paper for the cheapest apartment we could find. I found one for eighty dollars a month. That sounded good so I called the number listed and arranged to meet the landlady. She said it was on "something" and McAllister, but she needn't have been evasive. If she had told me the apartment was on Fillmore and McAllister, it wouldn't have meant anything to me. I had no idea that Fillmore and McAllister ("hype corner") was the worst corner in all San Francisco at that time. I wasn't even aware of the fact that there was such thing as a "bad" area.

Mrs. Perkins met us at her place on Geary. She smiled broadly when she opened the door, a woman in her mid-sixties dressed in conservative but shabby clothes. "Hello!" she beamed. "I'm Marge Perkins and I'm a Libra. What's *your* sign?" I was so taken aback I didn't know what to say. It was the sixties. People over thirty didn't ask that question then. "I'm sure you're going to love the apartment, and I *know* I'm going to like having such nice young people as tenants." She got her purse and we all three drove over to "something" and McAllister.

"This is great," I whispered to Sarah. "Only in San Francisco! Imagine, a woman in her sixties who asks about our signs and thinks we look like 'nice young people,' even with my beard and shoulder-length hair."

"Yeah," said Sarah. "I guess so. I guess it's great."

"What do you mean 'I guess'?" I said. "What's the matter?"

"Nothing," Sarah said. "It's great. I don't know . . . I guess it's great . . . She gives me a weird feeling though."

Mrs. Perkins let us into the apartment. It looked okay. I had never lived in an apartment; Sarah had never lived in anything else. I didn't know what questions to ask so I just let Mrs. Perkins talk.

"Now this will be *your* home, your own pad. You do your own thing here. If you want pets or want to have friends over, well that's just far out. I'm a Libra and Libras don't tell people what to do. You just do your own thing here." I had no idea landlords rarely allowed such things. Again I was charmed by Mrs. Perkins using expressions which, in those days, were new and exciting. "There's no lease. All I ask is first and last month's rent plus a forty-dollar cleaning deposit."

"What?!" I said, incredulous. "You want the last month's rent, too?"

"Easy, Eric," said Sarah. "That's standard for apartments."

"It is?" I asked. "Really?" Jesus, I was green. "Well, okay. We'll go cash the money order somewhere and bring back the two hundred dollars this afternoon." We had brought our entire nest egg, six hundred dollars, in a single money order. Jesus.

"Well . . . okay," said Mrs. Perkins, "but I can't guarantee the apartment will still be available this afternoon. If somebody else comes along with the cash I'll have to rent to them. You know

I'm a Libra; I've got to keep things balanced, be fair. It's only fair to rent to the first person who has the money in hand and I did have another call on it."

"It'll only take us a couple hours," I said. "Can't you wait that long?"

"Tell you what," said Mrs. Perkins. "You do seem like such nice young people. If you like you can endorse the money order over to me and I can give you a check for the difference."

"Ah . . . great!" I said. "I really appreciate that."

"Eric," Sarah whispered. "I'm not sure we should do this."

"How come?" I asked, genuinely surprised.

"I don't know," said Sarah. "I just don't like it."

"Well I don't see that we have much choice," I said. "You know I tried to cash this thing three times yesterday and nobody would do it. This way we get the apartment and we get the money order cashed too."

Mrs. Perkins wrote us a check for four hundred dollars and gave us a key. We then dropped her off at her place and went to a bank to open an account. And there her check bounced.

"What the fuck do we do now?!!" screamed Sarah. "That's all the money we had in the world! What are we going to do?!!" Sarah was panicked, beside herself. "I *told* you not to give her our money!"

"What do you mean you told me?" I snapped back. "All you said was you didn't like it. If you were so sure it was a bad idea, why did you let me do it?"

I learned something about Sarah Liebling that day. When she says "I don't like it," she is using the strongest language she can muster. When she says "I don't like it" she means "Don't, under any circumstances, do this." It took me years to learn this. Maybe I haven't learned it yet. I felt like a complete fool, and I knew that I had lost Sarah's respect.

"I don't know what to do," I said. "I guess we're fucked."

"Bullshit," she said. "You've got to get our money back."

"How?" I asked.

"Jesus Christ," Sarah growled. "We go back to Mrs. Perkins's place and make her give it back."

I knew that in order to get our money back I would have to have an ugly confrontation with Mrs. Perkins. I had never in my life been rude to an older person, but I knew that was what I would have to do. On my own I would have kissed off the money rather than have a confrontation, but I was bound and determined to get Sarah's respect back. We rode silently back to Geary.

"Your check bounced," I said to Mrs. Perkins when she opened the door.

"Don't be silly," she said. "I made a deposit this morning. Just take it back to the bank and have them check this morning's deposits." That sounded good to me. It was probably even true. I gave Sarah a sidelong glance. She stared straight at Mrs. Perkins.

"We want our money order back," Sarah said. "We want it now."

"Well I don't have it," Mrs. Perkins said coldly. "I deposited it. Now if you'll excuse me . . ." She backed away from the door and began to close it. Sarah shot me a do-something look.

Suddenly it was as if time slowed way down. I felt like I had plenty of time to think. If I let this woman close the door it would be like closing the door on my future with Sarah. I knew I had to do something, something completely out of character for me.

I shoved my foot between the door and the jamb, then I pushed the door open. "I want my money!" I yelled.

"I simply don't have it," Mrs. Perkins said, looking frightened.

I grabbed her by the front of her dress and pulled her face close to mine: a move I had only seen on television. "Give me my motherfucking money order," I said, "or I'll break your face." I couldn't believe I'd said that. I also couldn't believe how exhilarating it felt.

"Okay, okay!" she said. "Don't hurt me! Please don't hurt me!" To my surprise, she produced the money order. I had believed her when she said she didn't have it.

How many years ago was that? Fifteen? How many times have I lost and regained Sarah's respect since that time?

*

It was Sarah's idea to move to the country in 1980. She'd had enough of Seattle. Smaller than New York, less perverse than San Francisco, it was still a city and Sarah was looking for something new. Now she has her commercial organic strawberry patch, her garlic and herb patch, and her beef cows grazing in the pasture. Next year she is expanding into the cut flower business. She's never stopped her art work, and the galleries call often enough to keep her spirits up. She won't send the kids to preschool; she has enough to fill them up. The three of them tramp through hills and marshes every day, and all of them can easily spot the difference between a pileated woodpecker and a western grebe. In the fall they eagerly await the return of the snow geese and the rare trumpeter swans, and hope against all odds to once again get a glimpse of the diurnal snowy owl.

Me? I moved to the country hoping to leave my drug obsession behind, and yet my first act as a farmer was to plant a quarter of an acre of opium poppies.

I marvel at the change that's come over Sarah. She used to be such a moody ding-a-ling who couldn't even drive a car at thirty years old. Now, seemingly overnight, she's the one who can take care of business. I no longer seem to be able to cover even the minimal responsibilities. I haven't balanced the checkbook in months, and if I did I know it would come out wrong. I keep forgetting to send in the insurance payments, and neither car has had a tune-up since . . . I don't know. I call in sick nearly every Monday, and leave early two or three days a week. I forget to bring home duck food and chicken scratch, even though she reminds me every morning. Most days, I even forget my lunch. Drug addiction, say the experts, is progressive, incurable, and fatal. What can she do, except watch as the curse causes my gradual, inexorable deterioration, and prepare for the day when she will have to go it alone?

And things aren't much better at work. When I'm loaded, I do the work of three social workers; when I'm sick, I hole up in my office and do nothing. I still get things done, but how much longer can I keep that up? A guy in my line of work can't let himself go to hell. People are depending on me. If I worked in a swizzle stick factory it wouldn't matter so much if I couldn't work; but if I screw up, the ramifications can be disastrous. What would have happened if I had been strung out, unable to function, when I encountered Bob Downs?

I was a Children's Protective Services social worker when I met him, twenty-eight years old. I wasn't really clean. My slow relapse had begun, but I was only using once or twice a week: mostly pills I hustled from doctors, and exempt codeine cough syrup, the type you have to sign the book for. I wasn't hooked yet. I was working the downtown area of Seattle, investigating reports of abuse and neglect, trying to do what little a social worker can to protect kids from adults. I had learned quickly that most abusive parents are not bad people. They're pretty much like anybody else, trying to do their best to raise their children. Only in their case, their best isn't good enough.

Before I became a CPS worker I used to think I'd get this great satisfaction out of taking kids away from parents who mistreated them. I found, though, that I didn't. In most cases I felt as bad for the parent as for the kid. It's no fun to say to some poor bastard, "Hey man, your best just ain't good enough," and then cart his kid off to some shitty foster home where he won't be treated much better. But the case of Bob Downs . . . that was different.

Downs had an apartment on the northwest slope of Capitol Hill in Seattle, the area where most of the gay people live. My anonymous report said that Downs, an unmarried man, was sexually involved with his adopted fourteen-year-old son, Brian. I had no idea who had made the report, nor whether it was credible. I knocked on the door.

It took three or four minutes before Downs opened it. I could hear muffled voices and shuffling around inside. I figured he had seen my car through the window, a light brown Dodge with the words "Washington State Department of Social and Health Services" on the door. When he finally opened the door, it was only enough to peek through.

"Yeah?" he said.

"I'm Eric Detzer from Children's Protective Service," I said. "Are you Bob Downs?"

"Why do you want to know that?" he said.

"We received a report concerning your son Brian," I said. "I need to discuss it with you. We can talk here, if you like, or we can go down to my office; it's up to you." I already had a bad feeling about Downs. It's unprofessional as hell, but I had already made up my mind that something was wrong here.

"What kinda report?" Downs asked.

"It's a pretty serious matter," I said, "and I can't very well discuss it through a crack in the door. Do you want to talk about it here or downtown?"

Downs closed the door, unhooked the chain, and opened it wide. "All right—come on in," he said.

The inside of the apartment was strikingly impersonal. It looked for all the world like a motel. The furnishings were new and inexpensive. It looked like he had outfitted the whole place at K-Mart for under a thousand dollars. "Okay," he said, "talk."

Downs stood about five foot eight, maybe a hundred and sixty pounds. He had on Adidas, levis, a grey sweatshirt, and a baseball cap. He was wearing one of those digital wristwatches that have everything: time, date, stopwatch, calculator, and God knows what all. His sandy brown hair was neatly cut around the ears. Downs stood with feet firmly planted and his arms crossed. He appeared confident to the point of cockiness. He wasn't the slightest bit intimidated by me. He also didn't seem at all horrified by the fact that such an accusation had been made. Parents are usually devastated, incredulous. Bob Downs looked ready for a fight.

"Do you mind if I sit down?" I asked. He motioned toward the sofa. I sat down and pulled the referral sheet out of my briefcase. "Like I said, this is an anonymous report," I told him, "so I have no idea whether there's any truth to it. I'm here to find out. You want me to read it to you?"

"Sure," said Downs, still cocky.

"Okay," I said. "Let's see, 'Referrant indicates that Mr. Downs adopted Brian one year ago in Nebraska. They came to Seattle two or three months ago. Brian has not been attending school. Referrant further states that Brian has told several people about his sexual involvement with Mr. Downs and is apparently a willing participant in the relationship. Mr. Downs is currently working as an informant for the vice squad of the Seattle Police Department, providing information about boy prostitution."

"That's it," I said. "Is there any truth to it?" Downs gazed at me for a moment, then gave a snort-like laugh.

"It's true I'm an agent for the SPD," he said. "The rest of it's character assassination, probably called in by one of the punks I helped bust. It don't surprise me. This is the kind of thing that happens to agents when they're working under cover."

As soon as I heard Downs use the term "agent" instead of "snitch," I knew I had a valid report. Besides, I could *feel* that he was evil. A dark, chilling sensation came over me when he spoke. Talking to him was like talking to some of the slimy characters I'd known in San Francisco. You know how it is with some guys: his tone was steel; his eyes were dead. It was like he wasn't a member of the same species as other people. He was more like my uncle Vlad. He was a monster.

"Brian is adopted?" I asked.

"Uh-huh," said Downs. "You wanna see the papers?"

"Yes, I will," I said. "He was adopted in Nebraska?"

"That's right."

"And you've been here a couple, three months?"

"Right."

"Is Brian attending school?" I asked. It seemed crazy to keep avoiding the main issue, but I knew he was going to deny sex abuse, so I figured I might as well concentrate on the other stuff.

"He isn't in school yet," Downs said. "I'm involved in a major investigation. If I let Brian out of my sight he could be in danger, so I've got to keep him with me right now. The officers I work with told Brian and I to stick close together." (Bullshit, bullshit, bullshit.)

"Just what is it you do for the police?" I asked.

"We're going to break up Vinnie Brangaccio's little business," Downs said with a smirk. Before continuing he walked over to the window and opened it a crack. I could tell he only did this so that he would have to turn his back on me, showing the .45 automatic that was stuck in the back of his levis. "Big Vinnie controls all boys on Penney's corner. We're gonna bust him and his chickenhawks too." (Tough talk, Bob.) Chickens are pre-pubescent boys: those with no body hair. Hawks are the middle-aged men who lust after them. Penney's corner was the pickup spot in Seattle during the seventies. It's moved since then. "We've already got him worried," said Downs. "My associate seen him yesterday and he's worried."

"What part does Brian play in this?" I asked.

"Brian don't do nothing," said Downs. "He's not involved at all." Downs hiked up his trousers and patted his gun. He wanted to be *very* sure I knew he was armed.

"Is it true there's only one bed in the apartment?" I asked. I had to get to this sometime. You know, it's not all that easy to ask somebody if he's committing child abuse. It's hard to find the right words. It's damned awkward.

"Yeah," said Downs. "Brian sleeps on the couch." Well—that was a dead end. Nothing to do but come right out with it. "Is it true you're sexually involved with him?"

Bob Downs showed no affect at all, no anger, no indignation. He simply lapsed into an obviously prepared speech.

"That is a categorical untruth," Downs said. "My only involvement of a sexual nature has been involvement with females who are adult females. I'm not now, or have I ever been, involved in a sexual way with any male or with Brian." It doesn't take a Sigmund Freud to hear how falsely that rang. "I told you: this report was obviously made by a person or persons who are trying to take revenge on me. You check with Sergeant Jorgenson of the vice squad who'll tell you about the enemies I've made." (Right, Bob. Sergeant Jorgenson. I wondered what dirt Downs had on Jorgenson to make him so sure the sergeant would cover for him.) Downs's ersatz legal talk made him sound ridiculous as well as evil.

"Well, tell me this . . ." I began, but Downs cut me off.

"I'm not telling you nothing more," he said. "If you want more information you can address my attorney." He walked over to the door and grabbed the knob.

"That's fine," I said. "What's your lawyer's name?"

Downs hesitated. He obviously didn't have a lawyer. "Just talk to Sergeant Jorgenson," he said.

"No, I'm not going to talk to Sergeant Jorgenson," I said. "I'll talk to you. If you want a lawyer present, that's fine. But if you don't want to talk to me informally like this, I'll have to go over to the juvenile court and get a warrant to pick Brian up and place him in shelter care until I can complete my investigation." (Tough talk, Eric. If he wants to talk legal-eagle, we'll talk legal-eagle.)

Downs had opened the door, but now slammed it shut. "You don't know whom you're talking to, sonny boy," he said. "You're putting your job on the line, you know. I could have your job if you're not careful."

"I just want to find out what's going on," I said.

"Well there's nothing going on," he said. "And you're starting to piss me off." (Tough talk! Tough talk!)

"Let me just be sure I understand this," I said. "You've been in Seattle two or three months with an adopted child. This child has no bedroom in your home and does not attend school. He spends all his time with you because your work makes it too dangerous for him to be separated from you. So you take him with you while you're infiltrating the world of Big Vinnie and his boy prostitutes: a world that is so dangerous you have to be armed, even in your own home. Is that a pretty accurate picture?"

Bob Downs's face reddened and he clenched his fists. He began moving toward me. I felt my confidence begin to drain away. I'd been cocky too, feeling the power of the Department of Social and Health Services behind me. Now I was just Eric Detzer alone: a guy who'd never had a fight in his life. I was scared.

But I was also pissed. I couldn't stand this guy. I knew there was a lot more to the story than I had at that time. Later I learned that Bob Downs was working as a snitch to bring Big Vinnie down so he could replace him. He had gotten himself approved for adoption eligibility to cover the fact that he was a pimp and a chickenhawk. He was using Brian as a toy, exploiting this kid who had been rejected by his family, then shuffled around in foster care for years. I couldn't stand Downs and, scared as I was, I really wanted to hassle him.

"You better move your ass out of here, punk," Downs said.

"Yeah, I'm going," I said. "But I want to inform you that I've found sufficient grounds for a pickup order on Brian. I'll be back this afternoon with a warrant and uniformed police officers to take him into protective custody."

"You touch my kid and I'll find you, asshole," he said. "Then you're going to be sorry you fucked around with me. Now get the fuck out of here."

5

Secret of the Sangre de Cristos

Vlad Tepes was a terrible, brutal man. I like to pretend he was more like Count Dracula, the character Bram Stoker based on him. I wouldn't mind being related to a guy like that. Also I can see similarities between my infamous ancestor, the vampire, and me, the drug addict. In my fantasy Uncle Vlad looks like Bela Lugosi (who was an IV speed freak himself).

"Good evening, Mr. Harker," the Count said to the slightly shaken young man. "I am Vlad Tepes. Welcome to my little country."

"Good evening, Count Tepes," said Harker. "May I present my letters of introduction." He handed the Count an envelope, which was embossed with a large wax seal. The year was 1897.

"I'm sure everything is in order," said the Count with a half-smile. "I will not detain you while I read them; I'm sure you must be tired. It is a long trip from London, and travel in the Carpathians is wearisome to those not accustomed to it. You shall have rest and food before we talk. Leave your bags for my coachman and please to follow me."

Picking up a large candelabra, the Count motioned toward the staircase. Harker hesitated a moment, swallowing hard in a dry throat. The entry hall of Castle Tepes was huge and at one time had been splendid. Now it was dark and gone to ruin. Stones had caved in from large sections of wall, and thick dust covered everything. Years of spider webs had built up on the furnishings. The smell of dampness and decay was everywhere. A cold October wind blew into the room.

"Please forgive the condition of my ancestral home," said the Count in a voice that held no hint of embarrassment. "Mine is an ancient country, and a poor one. As you can see, even the nobility are unable to maintain even the pretense of wealth. This castle was built in a time when the furs and lumber of Transylvania brought high prices in the markets of Europe. Today, alas, the fur-bearing creatures are gone and the value of timber is a fraction of what it was."

"Quite a pity," said Harker nervously, unable to think of more to say.

"Yes . . . a pity," said the Count. "But I'm sure you will find your accommodations upstairs cheerful and cozy. If you will follow me, please." Harker fell into step behind the Count.

"And how do you like our primitive little country?" asked the Count as they slowly ascended the staircase. "Quite different from the hustle and bustle of your modern London."

"I daresay," replied Harker, beginning to relax a little. "I should think the England of King Arthur would have had more in common. Do you know that as I moved amongst the peasants today, they stared at me as though I were from the moon and kept making some sort of gesture at me with their hands. Do you suppose it was to protect themselves from the foreign demon?"

The Count chuckled. "Foreign demon? No . . . it was not to protect themselves. The gesture you mention was intended to protect *you*."

"Protect *me?*" said Harker, taken aback.

"My people, as I said, are primitive," said the Count. "They are riddled with fears and preposterous superstitions. By making the gesture you saw, they hoped to protect you from 'the evil eye'—the many ghosts and spirits they believe inhabit these mountains. Actually quite a hospitable act, don't you think?"

The Count pushed aside a great oak door, revealing a well-lit sitting room, comfortably furnished. It was clean and airy; Harker breathed a soft sigh. "I will leave you now to your rest," said the Count. "Your bags will be left outside your door presently. I will rejoin you for supper at midnight." With that, he closed the door and was gone.

"Well . . . what a queer bird," mumbled Harker. "I shouldn't like to be in his employ too often."

Tepes walked back down the staircase, picked up Harker's bags, and carried them to his guest's door. It was 10:30, not enough time to go out before his meeting with Harker. He hoped he hadn't given the Englishman too bad a scare. All his plans hinged on Harker doing exactly as he was told. And if his plans worked, he would finally be able to leave the Carpathians.

Ahh . . . to at last be away from the miserable Slovacs, Rumanians, Jews, and other trash. To at last be in a country where the name Tepes did not strike terror in the hearts of men. To reside in a city, where the occasional body found drained of blood would not be cause for concern. Tepes stroked his drooping mustache.

There was nothing to do until midnight, so Tepes did nothing. He simply stood in the hall and waited until the appointed hour. Tepes knew how to wait. After more than four centuries . . . he knew how to wait. He could wait now while this Saxon rested. Jonathan Harker, English solicitor and real estate agent, would find a suitable dwelling for him in London.

Count Vlad Tepes had inherited his title while still a young man. Educated, cultured, utterly autocratic, the youthful Count had had little actual contact with the people of his mountainous realm. Yet he took his responsibilities seriously—much like a keeper of good hunting dogs. It was his responsibility to care for them, protect them, and train them. But his subjects had turned out to be ignorant, ungrateful wretches, undeserving of his fidelity.

When the Ottoman Empire erupted out of Asia Minor and began spreading like a cancer across eastern Europe, Tepes knew his tiny country could not hope to withstand its might. He had virtually no standing army, and inadequate provisions for an extended siege. Transylvania was utterly vulnerable.

But young Vlad Tepes was clever. He ordered one hundred thousand peasants to be impaled on stakes. He then ordered the stakes placed every few yards along his entire border. The moans and cries of the dying could be heard for miles. When the Turks met this welcome they turned their columns and retreated.

"If this is what Transylvanians do to their own people," they said, "*we're* not going into battle with them. They can have their miserable, rocky little country."

Tepes was overjoyed; but to his everlasting surprise and chagrin, his people were not pleased with what he had done. Imagine! Here he avoided a war that would have claimed three times as many lives, and not just peasant lives, but nobles, merchants—valuable people. Cities and towns would have been burned. Crops would have been destroyed. He himself would have been deposed. But instead of honoring him for his cleverness, they cursed his barbarity. They called him murderer, Vlad the Impaler, and worst of all: "Dracula," the dragon.

*

The handle to Harker's door turned. Not wishing to be seen, Tepes closed his eyes in a moment of concentration. He drew his evening cloak around him and bowed his head. When Jonathan Harker tentatively peeked his head out, the hall was empty. He saw only dust, decay, and a large bat hanging from the ceiling.

"Bloody strange man," he murmured, laying hold of his suitcase and withdrawing into his room. "How can he live in such a Godforsaken place?"

Following the Turkish retreat, young Tepes withdrew entirely into court life where he would never have to have contact with the miserable common people. He spent his days attending to matters of state; evenings he read alchemy and geography, or listened to one of his three maiden cousins play. But outside the castle, rumors began to spread. It was whispered that demonic orgies took place at Castle Tepes. It was even said that the Count bathed in a tub of human blood each night. When he petitioned a neighboring noble for a wife, the father allowed the match only when Tepes offered a large sum of money. His bride was terrified of him, stayed away as much as possible, and sickened and died shortly after the birth of their first child.

One night in late fall, the bell of Castle Tepes was rung and a thin, pallid old man, looking ravished by disease, was presented to the Count. He identified himself as a relative, a wandering cousin returning to the family land. He had ancient documents with him that gave persuasive evidence that he was, indeed, a Tepes. The Count welcomed him respectfully.

"What brings you back to us, Uncle?" asked the Count. "Did you develop a nostalgia for our lovely Carpathians?"

"These mountains mean nothing to me," said the old man. "I am tired . . . and ready to face eternity. But before I succumb to death, I wish to pass on the secret of the Tepes family to the new liege."

"A family secret, Uncle?" said the Count. "I'm intrigued. I was not aware of any family secret. Tell me."

"Presently," said the old man. "You will know it presently. For now, I am tired. Please show me to my room."

The Count fell asleep shortly after midnight, but he awoke almost immediately. The fetid smell of his uncle filled his nostrils and he noted a faint tingling sensation at his throat. He felt relaxed – almost dreamy – and held very still until his uncle had removed his mouth from the Count's neck. As he gazed at his uncle, the Count realized there was an open wound on the old man's chest. Without thinking, Tepes placed his mouth over the wound, as he knew his uncle wanted, and sucked the warm, velvety blood into his mouth. He swallowed heavily several times before his uncle pushed him away rudely.

"Now – the secret has been passed on," said the old man. "I have walked the earth as long as I can bear; now it is you who shall see the passing of centuries. Now you are the *wampyr*. Then one day, when *you* can no longer bear it, you will pass it on to another member of our family."

"Is it only we, of this line, who may inherit this . . . honor?" asked the Count.

"Only we . . . yes, only we."

*

"Ah, Mr. Harker," said the Count. "I trust you have recovered somewhat from your long journey." The Count carried a large silver tray with covered dishes, which he put on a table near his guest. "The upstairs maid has been taken suddenly ill, so I must serve you myself. Please . . . eat with appetite."

"Thank you, Count Tepes," said Harker. "Are you not joining me?"

"I never sup," said the Count. "A meal a day sustains me; it has been my habit for many years."

"Well if you'll excuse me then," said Harker, "I'm quite ravenous and this smells delicious." He set to with knife and fork. "I say! This is marvelous. What sort of meat is it? It has such an unusual flavor?"

"It is baby . . . pig," said the Count. "An old recipe, and a specialty of my cook."

"Most unusual," murmured Harker as he devoured the food. The Count waited quietly.

*

Following the death of his wife, Vlad Tepes turned the care of his young daughter over to his three cousins. Sophie grew up in the castle, never being allowed to see or talk to anybody other than the Count and his cousins. A quiet and pensive child, she developed into a beautiful, dark, willowy young woman. The Count delighted in Sophie, though she did not return his affection and loyalty. She seemed always ill at ease and restless, taking long, solitary walks in the woods.

Three weeks after her nineteenth birthday, she went out for a walk and never returned. Tepes was enraged. When his own servants were not able to locate her, he had their feet and noses cut off, then retained a band of gypsies. He offered them a fortune if they could find her. The gypsies fanned out over the countryside; Tepes waited. Weeks passed, then months, then years.

Finally one of the gypsies returned with a young Jew whom the gypsy claimed knew about Sophie. The Count interrogated the boy himself and, by description, knew that it was indeed Sophie whom the infidel had known. His news was terrible. Sophie had slipped out of Transylvania disguised as a man and made her way to the Ukraine. There she had married a peasant, a farmer named Detzer. The Count, chained to his native soil each day, was unable to go after her.

That was hundreds of years ago. Just before Harker's visit, the Count had gotten news of Sophie's descendants. They had abandoned their family farm and drifted into what was now Finland. Finally they had sold everything and emigrated to America. As far as the Count knew there were no more members of the Tepes family left in Europe. Some day he would have to make his way to America and locate one of Sophie's descendants in order to pass on the family secret. But that would have to wait. Perhaps in a hundred years or so the mortals would invent faster conveyances, perhaps even one that could take him from Europe to America in a single night. For now, simply making his way to England presented sufficient difficulty.

★

"Will you have a cigar with your coffee, Mr. Harker?" asked the Count.

"Why yes, thank you," said Harker. "I must tell Minna about this excellent meal."

"Minna . . . that would be your wife?" asked the Count.

"Fiancée actually," replied Harker. "We're to be married as soon as I return from this trip."

"Ah, then we must conclude our business quickly so that you may return to her." The Count opened a case containing many documents. At that moment there was a loud howling of wolves just outside the window.

"My God!" said Harker, glancing toward the window. "They couldn't be more than ten yards away. Do they often come this close?"

"The wolves?" asked the Count. "Oh yes. I am quite fond of wolves. They are the children of the night I love so well. Listen – what music they make!"

Harker gave the Count a slightly horrified look. "But aren't you afraid that you might encounter them accidentally some time? They could rip a man to shreds in seconds."

"My dear Harker," said the Count. "Wolves do not attack – only defend. They have an integrity that exceeds that of humans."

The business with Harker was completed by four in the morning. The Count was pleased with the lawyer's find: a large estate gone to ruin, situated next to an insane asylum. His neighbor would be a psychiatrist, a Dr. John Seward. Harker was by this time quite exhausted, and the Count left him to retire. It being October, the dawn would not come for over four hours so the Count need not hurry overly much. He had enjoyed his conversation with Harker and, in truth, would have preferred to continue it. It had been so long since Tepes had had the opportunity to talk with an educated man. But Harker was tired and besides, it was necessary to hunt before the dawn.

The Count made his way down the hall and into his room. This was as dusty and decayed as the rest of the castle. On the table was a huge pile of gold coins and a large key ring. The Count passed quickly through the room, opened the window, and crawled, lizard-fashion, down the outside wall. The moon was near full and it illuminated the countryside through broken clouds.

When Tepes had first taken the secret from his uncle, killing had been a wonderful, exciting experience. Now, after centuries of repeating it, much of the thrill had gone. Killing had become primarily a necessity, less of a pleasure. He knew he must kill to survive, and at the moment of contact with his victim he still experienced excitement. Still, the constant *need* for killing had begun to wear on him over the past few decades. The Count was not always successful on his hunts. Sometimes he would return to the castle without having fed. On these occasions Tepes would be filled with anxiety, and arise the next evening panicked and desperate. He did not know how many days he could go without tasting blood. Two days? Three days? Perhaps four?

When he had made his way to the ground, Tepes again wrapped himself in his cloak, bowed his head, and went into a brief trance. Where he had stood, only a light mist remained. This mist drifted through the woods toward the river. Dawn was but two hours away and the Count knew that the younger villagers often chanced being abroad at this hour in order to be alone with their lovers. He soon located an amorous couple, locked in a passionate embrace.

The Count watched them, unseen. At first he decided to take the strong, healthy young man, but as he watched, the girl reached her orgasm. A blush of blood-filled passion glowed on her face, and a heavy vein throbbed between her eyes. Tepes changed his mind and decided on her. He waited for them to separate. The boy stood up.

"Where are you going, Ilya?" she asked, still flushed and breathless.

"I've got to pee," said Ilya, and he walked behind a tree in superfluous modesty.

In a twinkling, the mist was gone and Count Tepes grabbed the girl from behind, sinking his teeth into her neck and piercing the jugular vein. She made no sound, but Ilya seemed to sense trouble. He emerged from behind the tree, a baffling look of confidence on his face. Tepes was so startled by the boy's lack of fear he stopped his sucking to stare at him.

"Away . . . *Dracula!*" cried Ilya, his hand held high.

He dares insult me to my face, thought the Count. The boy is mad.

But suddenly the Count understood: Ilya held aloft a crucifix. Tepes smiled inwardly. For years he had, through his gypsies, circulated the rumor that the sight of this bauble would drive him away. Had the peasants not believed this myth, they would never have emerged from their dwellings at night. For reasons Tepes did not understand, he was unable to enter a human's home unless he was invited. As long as they thought they had some measure of protection, the intrepid ones would brave the night on occasion. The Count dropped the girl, sprang at Ilya, and with the strength of a vampire, snapped his neck. He then returned to the girl and finished draining her blood. The crucifix, he slipped into his pocket.

When the Count finished his feeding, he took an extra moment to reflect on this mortal body. With a bony, heavily-clawed finger he touched her breast, traced a line past her naval, then twined her blonde pubic hair. He inserted his finger in her vagina, which was well lubricated with female secretion and semen. "Mortals!" he mused. "They will risk so much for this silly need." Tepes could recall only dimly the urge to copulate. He had known only one woman, his wife, and the three or four times he had lain with her had been less than pleasant. Yet somehow he envied mortals this source of pleasure, now denied him for eternity. For no particular reason he ripped the arms, legs, and breasts off the girl, and the penis off the boy. He felt melancholy and returned quickly to the castle. There he shut himself into his ancient coffin and, haunted by a pervasive sense of discontent, he slipped toward oblivion.

"When I get to England," he mused, "things will be better."

★

The next evening Tepes ignored Harker. Yusef, the gypsy he employed, had brought news of Sophie's descendants in America.

"We have traced their progress from New York," said Yusef. "They made their way west, settling in a wild, desert area known as Colorado. His name is Gustaf. He has married, but has not yet fathered children. His wife is called Dolly. The family name is still Detzer. From Budapest it is a one-month journey."

"Ahh . . ." said the Count. "Too far for an undead traveler. It appears I must delay the passing of the secret for a while longer."

"I could accompany you, master," said Yusef. "I could protect you."

The Count chuckled. "My dear Yusef, you have been a valued servant, but my trust in you is no greater than your trust in me. I can wait, Yusef. I am quite good at waiting. Gustaf's child, or his child's child, will inherit my immortality. A few more years are as nothing to me."

But this was not entirely true. When the Count went out to feed, he found the hunt distasteful and the blood dissatisfying. As he looked ahead to the time it would take humans to invent jet airliners, he felt he could not bear to wait. He remembered the words of his uncle: "I am ready to face eternity." The Count, too, was ready to succumb to death—even if it meant eternal damnation.

Toward dawn Tepes returned to the castle and visited Harker.

"Count Tepes," said Harker. "I *am* glad to see you. I was beginning to get concerned that you'd abandoned me." Harker chuckled unconvincingly. He had meant his comment to sound facetious, but the truth of his fear had been obvious in his tone.

"My apologies," said the Count. "I had pressing business."

"I must say," Harker continued, "that I should think you'd die of loneliness out here in these mountains all alone."

"Die?" said the Count. "Of loneliness? No—I am not lonely. And as for dying—well, there are, Mr. Harker, worse things than to be dead."

*

My Dad never spoke about his early years in Colorado. When he told stories of his boyhood they were always about Hollywood. He must have been about Rose's age when Gus and Dolly moved the family to California. Still, at some point little Bud must have sat on the front porch of the cabin in Colorado, watching the sun rise over the Sangre de Cristo Mountains.

I've never been back to the Phoenix suburb where I grew up. Today they call it "the Town That Millionaires Built," but back in the fifties when my family moved there, it billed itself as "the

West's Most Western Town—Where Horses Have the Right of Way." It was pretty ordinary. There was a soda fountain at Lute's Drugstore where we used to hang out. Then they built a mall with a Basha's Supermarket, and we changed our hangout to Ryan/Evans. I got clothes at Saba's and footwear at Goot's Shoes. No matter where I went I ran into kids I knew. We all went to Kiva Elementary. We all delivered the Scottsdale *Daily Progress.*

I hear things about Scottsdale that surprise me. Some company even makes a pickup truck called Scottsdale; I can't imagine why. The town must be quite different now.

But I don't want to go back. I don't want to see how it's changed, just as I don't want to see how I've changed. I don't want to go back, but then again, I don't want to spend the rest of my life just sitting here, waiting for Uncle Vlad.

For the past few years, it's been the same every year. I pass through the House of Mirrors in the late fall, suffer in the House of Blue Lights all winter and part of spring, then in May the little plants start to come up. I always tell myself I'm not going to get strung out again this year, but I always do.

And so it begins again. Ranging over the countryside in the middle of the night, looking for early bloomers. My own crop comes in about July, and no matter how much I grow I never have enough to store any away. By September my stuff is gone and I'm out in the night once again.

Uncle Vlad has been ravaging the darkness for nearly five hundred years. He's sick of it. I know he's thinking about me, making plans to catch an SST over the pole from London. If he were to come in November, he could leave England at dusk, land at Sea-Tac International around midnight, rent a car, drive up Interstate 5, and be waiting by the barn for me when I get back from one of my raids. Then I'd be up shit creek without a paddle for all eternity.

I gotta do something.

6

My Brother's House

"My name is Eric Detzer," I told the receptionist. "Ted Schimmle from Skagit County Mental Health Center called you about me. At least, he said he was going to call." The receptionist didn't say anything; she just kept looking at me. "Did Ted call you about me?" I couldn't tell if the expression on her face indicated that she was baffled, irritated, or just patient. "He said I should come here today at ten. Is that right?"

"He called us," the receptionist said at last. "You'll be seeing Cindy Olsen first, then Dr. Taber at eleven. Did you bring the money? Ted explained to you that we'd have to have two hundred fifty dollars up front, right?" Ted had indeed explained this to me and it had come as no surprise that an agency that deals with drug addicts, even middle-class, white-collar addicts such as I am, would want payment in advance.

"Yes, I have the money," I said. "But my insurance will pay a substantial portion of this."

"That's all right," said the receptionist, whose name was LaWanda. "When they pay their share we'll credit it to your account." She became noticeably friendlier after I had written the check. "Ted's referral letter arrived the day before yesterday and Cindy and Dr. Taber have had a chance to review it. Just take a seat and they'll be with you in a moment. Want a cup of coffee?"

I had a copy of Ted's referral letter in my pocket. I had read it a dozen times:

December 10, 1984

Cynthia Olsen, M.S.W.
Health and Treatment Services Northwest
Cabrini Towers Bldg.
Seattle, WA

Dear Ms. Olsen:

I am writing to refer Mr. Eric Detzer (DOB 8.4.48) who has been in treatment with me for the past fourteen months. Mr. Detzer came to me requesting help with an unusual type of drug problem. He is addicted to the raw extract of the opium poppy plant—a variety grown ornamentally around the Puget Sound area. Despite a high degree of motivation to change his maladaptive behavior, and a high level of social functioning (he is a psychiatric social worker), Mr. Detzer has been unable to maintain himself in a drug-free state for more than a few weeks at a time. Thus far his longest period of total abstinence has been twenty-seven days. When off opiates he reports moderate to severe anxiety, dysphoria, and pervasive anhedonia.

Our psychiatrist, Michael Lundbeck, M.D., was consulted and treatment for depression was begun. Mr. Detzer was tried on a variety of tricyclic antidepressants and, when satisfactory results were not achieved, he was tried on a monoamine oxidase inhibitor. This too failed to provide any substantial relief from symptoms.

It is the feeling of the Skagit Mental Health Center that we are not able to provide effective treatment to Mr. Detzer at this time and therefore are making this referral in the hope that Health and Treatment Services Northwest can provide the help he has not been able to receive here.

Enclosed please find copies of our clinical records. If I can be of further assistance, please do not hesitate to call.

Sincerely,
Theodore L. Schimmle
Chemical Dependencies Specialist

The referral wasn't Ted's idea. He was perfectly willing to keep right on trying. But as I looked at my stash and realized I had only about a week left, and as I thought about what it would be like to go through the House of Mirrors again, something snapped. "I can't do it again, Ted," I said. "I don't have another cold turkey left in me. I'm tired, man. I want methadone. Even if it means driving to Seattle, I want methadone."

"Cindy will see you now," LaWanda said, and motioned me back toward the office. I stubbed out my cigarette, took a last swallow of coffee, and swung my jacket over my shoulder. I could see Cindy Olsen, MSW, standing in the hall. She was tall, slender, and to my mind overdressed and overly made-up. I guessed her to be ten years my junior.

"Hello Eric," she said. "I'm Cindy Olsen and I'm a social worker."

"So am I," I said, probably a little too sarcastically.

"Hmmm, so you are," said Cindy, leafing through my chart. She gave an ironic little laugh and changed the subject.

"I'll be seeing you first to get a history. Then you'll meet with Dr. Taber. He should be here in about an hour or so."

I'm sure Cindy had no idea how devastated I felt by this statement. I had taken no opiate for over twenty-four hours; I was in Stage Four withdrawal. The idea of having to wait another hour to see the doctor, whose magic right hand would write the order that would finally end my suffering, was almost more than I could bear. I had not slept the night before. I had sat in my Dad's easy chair thinking to myself, "nineteen hours, twenty-seven minutes; eleven hours, four minutes; six hours, forty-three minutes; two hours, nine minutes, twenty-one seconds." Now I would have to add another hour, maybe more, to this interminable timetable. I didn't want to talk to a social worker. I didn't want to talk about my "problem." I wanted methadone. I wanted relief. If I had thought talking would do any good I would have stuck with Ted. But I'd been around long enough to know the two cardinal rules of dope peddling, whether it's quarter-teas of heroin or doses of methadone:

Number one: Always make your buyer provide cash up front.
Number two: Always make him wait.

I knew that, no matter how bad I felt, I *was* going to spend an hour with Cindy, and when that was over I'd have to wait even longer for Dr. Taber to show up. When he finally did arrive, I would probably have to spend an inordinate amount of time with him.

"It must be pretty difficult for you to come in here," Cindy said, "pretty embarrassing. Do you feel terribly uncomfortable?" She had such an intense, serious look on her face that I almost laughed. She was assuming that as a professional, a colleague, I would find it humiliating to be seeking treatment for drug addiction. I could see she felt badly for me.

"I'm uncomfortable because I'm in *withdrawal,*" I said. "Whatever professional embarrassment I may have felt is long since over. Right now I don't care what anybody thinks of me. I'm tired, I'm beaten, and I'm sick as a fucking dog. I'm glad as hell to be here."

Cindy pulled out a yellow legal pad and began the tedious process of getting a "history." She wanted me to tell her the entire story of my life as a drug addict—a story which was a full seventeen years long. I was sick and miserable, but I knew Health and Treatment Services Northwest was not going to come up with a single milligram of methadone until they had the whole story—from 11th between A and B up to the present. I sweated, I burned, I wrung and twisted my hands, but I told the story.

"Okay," said Cindy. "You got out of the hospital, you and Sarah got back together, and you moved to Seattle. Then what happened?"

"I got a job as a counselor in a drug-abuse program," I said, "and Sarah went to school at the University. I worked there for several years. Evenings and weekends I went to class and managed to finish my bachelor's degree. Then I cut back to half-time work and went to graduate school full-time. Sarah was also doing postgraduate work. When I finished my master's degree I went to work as a children's protective service worker."

"You mean you investigated child abuse?" asked Cindy. "That sounds pretty heavy. Was it?"

"No—it was okay," I said. "I liked it. I did it for three years: 1978 to 1980."

"Yuck," said Cindy. "I don't think I could do that."

Every time I tell somebody that I used to work for a children's protective service, they always answer that way. I feel like I could say the words right along with them: "I (I) couldn't (couldn't) do (do) that (that)." Everybody thinks it sounds so horrible, but it wasn't. Oh, I had a hard time with the murders, and the burn injuries were hard to bear, but mostly I liked it. I liked the feeling that I was doing something truly important and necessary, even if it didn't pay much. No type of social work pays well, unless you're a therapist at Esalen or something.

"So when did you start using drugs again?" Cindy asked.

"Let's see," I said. "I got out of the hospital in '71, moved to Seattle in '72. My dad died in '74. I think I started chipping around about then."

"Taking heroin?" she asked.

"Christ no," I said. "I haven't used heroin since I left San Francisco. I started up again by drinking over-the-counter codeine cough syrup, the kind you have to sign the book for. There was this big drugstore in Seattle on First Avenue near Pioneer Square—Henderson's. They had three pharmacists. At 9:00 they'd open the doors and let all us scumbags in. One of the pharmacists would yell, 'All right, form a line to the left and have your IDs ready.' You were allowed to buy one four-ounce bottle every seven days. I'd sit around with my thumb up my butt all week. Then every Friday at 9:01 A.M. I'd walk into Henderson's, buy my bottle, and down the whole thing in one gulp."

"And how long did that go on?" Cindy asked.

"A long time," I said. "A couple of years. Long enough that I began to believe that I wasn't going to get readdicted. And in fact I probably wouldn't have, if the Board of Pharmacy hadn't closed Henderson's down and I hadn't learned to grow and harvest opium. It was learning to grow it that finally put me back on the road to the Monkey House."

"And how long have you been using opium?" she asked.

"Heavily? About five years. As long as I was slitting pods I didn't do it every day. It wasn't until I learned to make a tea out of it that it really got out of hand, because then I was able to steal plants from other people's yards, which gave me a virtually unlimited supply for three-quarters of the year."

"And the winter months?" she asked.

"You're going to find this hard to believe," I said, "but those decorative dried poppies that they sell in florist supply stores are the same stuff. Drying them doesn't affect the opium. It's still in there, still water soluble."

"You buy opium from florists?" Cindy asked, incredulous.

"Mmm hmm," I said. "Florists."

"You know, Eric," said Cindy. "This is all pretty hard to believe. I mean, I can see that you're in withdrawal; there's no doubt you've been using opiates and using them heavily, but this business about poppies – well, it's just hard to believe. I've been in this business five years and I've never run across a poppy addict before. Tell me the truth now, are you really strung out on poppies, or are you covering something?"

"You see, Cindy," I said. "This is why it's taken so long to come in for treatment. I knew this would happen. I knew it would be nearly impossible for me to get people to believe my story. All my friends know I grow poppies and make a tea out of them, but none of them believe there's 'real' opium in there."

"These are drug-using friends?" Cindy asked.

"No, my friends don't use drugs. Most of them don't even drink. I haven't known drug users for years," I said.

"Well," said Cindy. "I don't see that I have much choice other than to believe you. It's weird, but if you say you're a poppy addict – okay." Cindy took off her glasses, laid her pen down, and closed the folder. She gave me a long, quizzical look. "I just have one more question," she said, "and that's *why*. Why now? Why are you here for treatment? You don't have any legal charges; you're not in trouble at work; you've got no family pressure to stop. What made you decide to come in?"

"Because I'm sick of it," I said.

"No," said Cindy. "Nobody ever stops for that reason alone. There's always something else, some external reason. What's yours?"

"It's Uncle Vlad," I said. "If he catches me out at night I'll be fucked for all eternity."

"Huh?" said Cindy. "What are you talking about? Who's Uncle Vlad?"

"Never mind," I said. "It's not important."

*

I had a dream last night. I dreamed I was in the suburban town where I grew up, except that the whole town was under a gigantic roof, like a shopping mall. I was climbing around on some large, plastic viaducts when I ran into a woman I know who owns a sandwich shop in Seattle. Her name is Miriam. Miriam is not pretty, but somehow I have always had an unexplainable attraction to her. In the dream I encountered Miriam counting money. She had lots and I wanted it. She could see me looking hungrily at her stacks of bills, and she started to laugh. This made me so mad I grabbed her by the throat and said, "If you don't shut up, I'll rape you!" Miriam laughed even harder so I threw her on the ground with her arm twisted behind her back. I pulled up her dress from behind and held her to the ground. She laughed and laughed. Furious, I spat in my hand and rubbed the saliva between her buttocks, inserting a moistened finger in her rectum. I then spat again, wetting my erection, and raped her anally. This brought uproarious laughter from Miriam.

"Is that it?" she said. "Man, I felt your finger more than this!"

I became overcome with rage and produced a razor-sharp fishing knife from somewhere. I dragged it hard across her neck, severing jugular vein, carotid artery, and tracheal tube. Miriam's laughter bubbled and gurgled through the blood which now ran in torrents over our bodies, and she died as I ejaculated onto the sweat-soaked sheets of my bed.

The nightmares that occur during early withdrawal are often prurient and disgusting. They are not the dreams of St. Francis of Assisi.

★

I didn't live at home in Phoenix when I was in high school; I went to that egghead boarding school up north. But I had to spend summers at home. Teenagers are perennial malcontents anyway, and I was particularly so. I wasn't used to living with my parents. Sometimes I would get so bored and antsy I thought I might lose my mind. At those times I would borrow my father's car and whip over to L.A. to visit my brother. Steve worked long hours and had never married, so I had the place to myself. I could do whatever I wanted. I could stay out all night or sleep all day or just sit on the beach and watch the surf. Now the truth is, I could do those kinds of things at home too, but somehow it wasn't the same. When I was at my brother's house, I felt free and unencumbered. I felt the way I imagined a grown-up felt. I *was* a grown-up; except I didn't have to pay rent, cook, or answer to anybody. It was a wonderful feeling and I loved my brother's house, even though I always knew it was temporary.

So Health and Treatment Services Northwest gave me a new House to add to my neighborhood. It was methadone maintenance and I called it, of course, My Brother's House. It was wonderful. I floated through the holidays like the ghost of Christmas past; I hardly remember them. The terrible month of January, usually so cold and dull, flew by in a twinkling. And February . . . what happened to February? It seems to have come and gone without my notice. One day is so much like another when I'm in My Brother's House.

★

I should have known that when Cindy Olsen, MSW, was finished with me I would have to go through the whole thing again for Dave Taber, MD. It had taken Cindy a solid hour to get through her "history." Then I had to sit in the waiting room another thirty minutes waiting for the doctor. When I was finally called into the exam room and seated across the desk from him, he wanted to go all the way back to 11th between A and B . . . again. I ached, I burned, I sweated . . . but I wanted that methadone. I told the story again.

"Seventeen years," said Dave. "That's a long time to be strung out. It's amazing you've been able to hold your life together as well as you have."

"Not really," I said. "It's a lot easier to keep it together when your stuff grows in the garden, when you don't have to hustle for it."

"Still, you've held yourself together remarkably well," Dave said. "So well that *I* don't think you're a candidate for methadone."

I stiffened and paled. "What did you say?" I whispered through clenched teeth.

"I don't think you're a candidate for methadone," Dave said, "and I'll tell you why. Methadone is a good drug for people who have messed up their lives so much that they need the time to put things back together. You've got a good job, you're maintaining a stable family, and you're not in trouble with the law. You don't really need methadone. Now, there's a relatively new treatment for detox, a drug called clonidine, which controls most of the worst withdrawal symptoms. A couple of weeks on that and you could be drug-free."

"I want methadone, Dave," I said in a soft, tense voice.

"Clonidine was discovered by accident," Dave continued, ignoring my statement. "It's really an antihypertensive and still its primary use is to control high blood pressure. A few years ago an internist happened to prescribe it to a narcotics addict who also had hypertension. Within a few days it became clear that not only did it stop his high blood pressure, it also made his narcotics withdrawal a piece of cake. We've used it on dozens of addicts here and the results have been amazing. I had one guy, a real hard-core junkie, who stopped heroin cold, took clonidine, and never even missed one day of work. It's great stuff and I think you ought to give it a try."

"No," I growled. "I want methadone. I came here for methadone, I've spent thirty-six hours in withdrawal so I could get methadone, and that's all I want."

"And I'm telling you that you should try clonidine," Dave said.

I could feel the frustration and rage that had been building in me begin to bubble up and boil over. I was nearly torn apart with the agony of drug craving and I had had it with the blathering of these two morons. I raised my clenched fists over my head and brought them smashing down on his desk.

"Listen you fucking asshole!" I screamed. "You can take your clonidine and shove it up your ass! I came here for methadone and methadone is all I want. If you're willing to give it to me, great. If not, say so, so I'll get out of here and go cop. But for Christsakes shut up about this fucking clonidine!"

Dave Taber, MD, gave me a long, sad look. "Okay, Eric," he said. "I'll play it any way you like. It's certainly better to take methadone than go on using the way you have. You want methadone . . . you got it."

"No shit?" I said.

"No shit."

I then gave Dave a long look, and I realized something I had not noticed before. I scared him. Dave and I were the same age and clearly hailed from very similar backgrounds. We had both been "golden boys" during our youth: bright, ambitious, well liked. We even had the same type of look: long hair, mustaches, stylish sport coats and trousers. Dave saw something in me that struck terror in his heart.

"It's just the luck of the draw," he said. "The situation could just as easily be reversed. You could be sitting on this side of the desk and I could be over there. None of us is invulnerable. We get physician addicts who come here for treatment. If it can happen to them, and to you, it could happen to me or anybody else. It could happen . . . and it scares the shit out of me—you know?"

"I think we'll start you out on sixty milligrams a day," he said. "If it's not enough, give us a call in a couple of days and we'll talk."

"That should do it," I said, secretly thrilled. I had been hoping for forty, willing to settle for thirty. Suddenly all the waiting, all the arguing, all the hassle seemed worth it. Sixty milligrams. I rolled the number silently around in my mouth. Sixty milligrams. A normal maintenance dose is usually forty. Dave walked me down to the lobby and into the pharmacy on the first floor, which was specially licensed to dispense methadone. The Chinese druggist poured six ten-milligram tablets into my hand. I looked at them for just a moment. On the street methadone sells for up to two dollars a milligram. I was holding nearly one hundred twenty dollars' worth of stuff in my hand. With a quick flip of my wrist I tossed all six tablets into my mouth and downed them with a sip of water.

"That'll be $2.85 for today," said the pharmacist. "From now on your dose will be prepared over at the Center for Addiction Services and you'll get it in a bottle mixed with Kool-Aid; then it'll be $1.50."

"It'll take us a week or so to get FDA approval to have your dose dispensed at Skagit General Hospital," said Dave. "Until then you'll have to drive down here for it each day. Did you make a follow-up appointment with Cindy?"

"I'm seeing her Thursday," I said.

"Well, if you have problems between now and then just give a holler," said Dave. "Good luck, my friend." We shook hands.

Four hours later I sat at my desk at work, staring out the window, a feeling somewhere between despair and panic lurking just outside my consciousness. My sixty milligrams was just barely holding me. I was no longer in withdrawal, but the nose-itching, eyelid drooping high I had been expecting had not materialized. I was not sick, but I most certainly was not loaded.

"My God," I thought. "I have a bigger habit than ninety percent of the heroin addicts shivering on the corner of 23rd and Madison. I'm more strung out than the hypes who are still copping milk sugar bullshit on 125th and Lexington. I've done something pretty bad to myself."

Jesus.

7

Of Monsters and Madmen

Sarah stomped the brake, skidded on the gravel, and lay a half-brodie in the driveway. "Who's Cindy?!!" she screamed.

I had been standing on the back porch for about forty-five minutes, waiting for her. My dope fiend's sixth sense had been tingling. Somehow I knew there was going to be some kind of trouble. I'd been in treatment at Health and Treatment Services Northwest for five weeks, taking methadone daily and driving to Seattle once or twice a week to see Cindy for counseling. I knew I wouldn't be able to hide it from Sarah forever, but I could never seem to find a good time to tell her.

"Somebody named La *Waaaanda* called to say that 'Cindy' won't be able to see you tomorrow," said Sarah, her voice quivering with barely controlled rage. She pushed open the car door and lurched out. "Now who the fuck is Cindy?"

"She's a drug abuse counselor in Seattle," I said, my voice calm and flat. I still hadn't made up my mind to tell Sarah the truth. This new wrinkle in the saga of my addiction seemed just too much. Different options were flying around in my head: Cindy's a counselor making a referral to the Gateway program, a graduate student who wants my consultation on a research project, a friend of a friend with a schizophrenic brother, an applicant for a job that's opening up in the Department, a former classmate who wants me to write a letter of recommendation. Cindy's nobody, nobody important.

"Who *are* these people . . . why are they calling at my home?" Sarah asked.

"Why don't you come inside," I said, "and I'll tell you about it."

"I don't want to go inside," Sarah said, steaming. "I want you to tell me why people I don't know are calling for you at my house."

"Cindy is a counselor," I said, deciding to go with it, "a drug abuse counselor, *my* counselor."

"What do you mean *your* counselor?" asked Sarah, the anger draining from her voice.

"Just that," I said. "She's my counselor."

"You're not seeing Ted any more?" she asked.

"Ted referred me to Cindy. She's in Seattle at a methadone program."

"You're on methadone?" asked Sarah, incredulous.

"That's right," I said. "I've been on it for five weeks."

Sarah looked at me, her mouth open slightly, and I could see her shifting gears. Her anger gave way to indignation. She looked down at the ground, spit in the gravel, and very deliberately stepped on the saliva and ground it into the dust. She pulled out a cigarette, saw that it was broken, so returned it to her pocket.

"Jesus Christ," she said, not looking at me. "You're on methadone and you didn't tell me." It was a statement, not a question.

"That's right," I said. "Now come on inside, will you? Let me tell you the story." I turned and walked back toward the house. Sarah hesitated a moment, unsure what to make of things, but eventually followed me in. I sat stiffly at the kitchen table and danced my fingers. Sarah slowly pulled a chair out and studied it for a moment. I could see that the process of shifting gears was almost complete. She sat down.

"You want me to make coffee or something?" I asked, but Sarah just shook her head. "Okay," I said. "Here goes. I wasn't able to do it . . . you know? I mean, the summer ended, I had a hundred-and-fifty-pod-a-day Jones, and . . . well, I just couldn't do it. I tried, but I don't know, I guess I cracked. I tried to wait it out like before, but somehow I lost confidence that the awfulness would ever end. I got convinced that I'd feel like shit for the rest of my life." Sarah didn't say anything; she just kept looking at her hands. "It's hard to explain," I continued. "I lost control of it. I could stay clean for a few days and then . . . wham! . . . off I'd go, without being able to stop myself.

"I've been bitching about my poppy tea habit for so long I knew you were sick of it. I knew another relapse would be more than you could handle. So I figured I'd try to do it on my own, keep it secret, not involve you in it this time."

"You were trying to protect me?" asked Sarah.

"Yeah, something like that," I said.

Sarah stood up and walked to the sink. She rinsed out a sponge and brought it over to the table. She wiped the crumbs to the floor. "But you did involve me," she said. "I mean—what's the point? You try to do this big, manly thing, but it doesn't work. These things never work. And by the time I do get involved, it's in a way that jacks me around twice as much as if you'd just told me to begin with."

"I know, I know," I said miserably. "I was afraid you'd be mad, that you wouldn't understand."

"Well, you're right about that," Sarah said, laughing without a trace of mirth. "And I have had it with this stuff. It's one thing to go crazy like this when you're twenty, but you're getting close to forty, and you've got kids who're depending on you. What are you doing still playing junior gangster at your age?"

(When I was a child, said Paul of Tarsus, I talked like a child, I thought like a child, I reasoned like a child. When I became a man, I put childish things behind me.)

The only way I could answer her was: "What can I say? You're right. I don't have any way to justify myself."

"Then why do you keep doing it?" she snapped.

"I don't know," I said. "Honest to God I don't know. Sometimes I think the only way to stop myself is to take my life." The instant those last words slipped out I regretted them. I had not intended to let Sarah know I was contemplating suicide. I myself cannot tolerate people who threaten suicide, and I'd been in the mental health business long enough to have heard hundreds of such threats. Sarah's reaction was not so different from what my own would have been if the tables had been turned.

"That's very dramatic," she said. "And I'm sure it shows what a mean bitch I am that I don't feel sorry for you. But, Jesus Christ, come on. I've got problems of my own—all I can handle. I don't have the energy to deal with yours, too."

I walked to the window and, standing there, put my forehead to the glass. I felt empty. I knew I had lost control of my addiction and that my only chance was to go through with treatment. But I also knew that, without a lot of support from Sarah, treatment was unlikely to be effective. And she had made it clear that my many past relapses had exhausted my credit.

"I love you, Sarah," I said without looking at her.

"Can you see how that's hard for me to believe?" she asked. "I mean, what you do speaks louder than what you say."

"I know you're right," I said, "but can you see how getting treatment can be a way of saying I do care about you?"

"I can see how treatment can be a way of getting *methadone,*" Sarah said cruelly. I winced. It was an unfair thing to say. There was also some truth in it.

⋆

I spent six years in college studying psychology, and I've practiced the art now for thirteen years. A lot of people have written a lot of stuff in this field, yet to my mind only two men in the history of western civilization really have known anything about human beings and the way we do things. The first was Moses who, in the Pentateuch in general and the Book of Genesis in particular, told the stories that held the germ of knowledge. The second was a poet whose name has been lost: the author of the epic poem *Beowulf.* Freud and the others came and went, but their efforts turned out to be unnecessary at best, and harmful and misleading at worst. At work, I have a tendency to let myself get carried away with issues such as coping abilities, social skills, interpersonal relations, and impulse control; but in truth there is only one issue in psychology—the conflict between good and evil.

It's not considered proper form to use the words "good" and "bad" in psychology today. Psychotherapists invariably opt for the nonjudgmental terms "adaptive" and "maladaptive." We don't want maladaptive patients to think of themselves as bad; rather, we want them to see themselves as . . . what? . . . out of step? . . . self-defeating? Something like that. And I think that's fine. I've got no business judging somebody else. The problem is that we in the profession have begun to evaluate ourselves in the same terms. And as a result we have begun to fuck ourselves up by looking at *ourselves* in the style of dummies like Carl Rogers or Leo Buscaglia, and ignoring the truly wise of history. Drug addiction is not maladaptive. It is bad, evil, and just plain wrong. It is a sin.

I am a namer of things and so, of course, I have a name for the monster inside me who takes control of my consciousness, overpowers my will to stay clean, and drives me out into the night in search of opium. The monster's name is Grendel.

Long before there were any such designations as "Europe" or "Scandinavia," back when Christianity was young and Paul had only recently wandered into Damascus, there were tribes of human beings in the northeastern part of the western hemisphere who were little more than animals. A legend emerged from the mead halls of these barbarians about a great, hairy monster, coated with loathsome slime and reeking of rotted flesh, who terrorized their villages and devoured great numbers of people. Grendel was a beast of terrifying strength who fed not only on thanes, but also bear, oxen, and an occasional whale. He was thought to be invincible until the day a hero, a Geat called Beowulf, arrived by sea to challenge the evil monster. Though he was big as a mountain and powerful beyond belief, the Danish thanes scoffed at Beowulf's boast that he would do battle with the dread Grendel and vanquish him. But Beowulf demonstrated that there was more to "strength" than stout spears and sharp swords, and the very day he arrived from across the water, the monster Grendel met his bloody end.

Plenty of Danes had tried to stand up to Grendel over the years. See, it wasn't just that the monster killed and ate people; it was also that he kept them from using Heorot, the fancy new mead hall that King Hrothgar had built for the thanes so they could let the good times roll. Grendel hated good times. He howled and moaned in fury every time he heard people having a good time. So Hall Heorot was his favorite place to snatch people. Proud, arrogant warriors would draw sword and spear, and would be plucked up and eaten like ripe apples.

In the Narcotics Anonymous book (what they call the "black book") there is an admonition that I've always thought remarkable, both for its truth and its simplicity. It is: "Insanity is repeating the same mistakes and expecting different results."

Beowulf left his sword on the beach when he arrived in Daneland. Swords had never been of much use against Grendel. Hrothgar and the boys at Hall Heorot thought Beowulf was nuts, yet they had to admit that indeed nobody had had much luck with weapons. So they threw a big daytime feast for the visiting Geats, whooping it up like crazy to be sure they pissed Grendel off. Then as darkness came, all the Danish thanes split and left Beowulf and his band in the hands of God.

The Geats were tired from the long trip and all the mead. One by one they fell asleep until only Beowulf remained awake. He waited. King Hrothgar couldn't sleep. Queen Wealthow only dozed. The night wore on. Fog rolled in from the sea. Mist drifted out from the marshes to the east. It was cold. Still Beowulf waited.

In the hour before dawn a sickening stench made Beowulf gag and cough in the darkness. He turned his head just as the huge, iron-reinforced doors of Heorot exploded off their hinges.

Grendel had arrived.

A sleeping Geat quickly disappeared into the jaws of the foul monster; his blood ran on the floor of the hall. Grendel had grown cocky and confident over the years. He didn't even notice that one of the Geats wasn't sleeping, that this Geat was in fact moving toward him. Grendel reached for another victim . . . *whomp!* Beowulf grabbed him by his hairy, slimy arm and hung on. Grendel shrieked and howled, but he had been caught off guard. Beowulf twisted the arm behind the monster's back, gave a mighty jerk, and pulled it right out of its socket. Oceans of black, fetid blood spewed out of Grendel's shoulder and the surprised, mortally wounded beast turned and ran from the hall.

Beowulf knew that you don't get rid of monsters by trying the same thing, over and over, year in and year out—spears and swords, swords and spears. He also knew that giving up, deciding to just try to live with a monster is not living at all. It's bullshit. You must get rid of monsters, and if swords and spears don't do the trick, you try something else. To the Danes, Beowulf seemed insane going against Grendel bare-handed, but in fact it was the Danes with the weapons who were insane. Insanity is repeating the same mistakes and expecting different results.

⋆

The daffodils are blooming! The famous daffodil fields of western Washington's Skagit Valley. Hundreds of screaming yellow acres checker the county. Winter is over. The migrants are here in their vans full of kids to pick the flowers.

In eight days I will be taking my final dose of methadone. The ninety days in My Brother's House are all but over. I already feel the familiar signs of the House of Mirrors. My left leg aches, just above the knee. There is a tickle in my throat which becomes a gag if I cough. The runs are back, and so is my own peculiar symptom: the burning bone marrow. I was supposed to use this time to "prepare" for kicking. I'm not sure if I've done it. I've gone to see Cindy religiously, but it's hard to know if that's done any good. Cindy is five months pregnant and I don't think she wants to think about dope fiends right now. I've gone to Narcotics Anonymous meetings, but while I've been on methadone they've seemed kind of dumb. I've revealed myself to a few friends, but they all think methadone is sort of like antabuse and still have trouble taking me seriously. Sarah is sick to death of hearing about it.

I'll miss old Guy the pharmacist at the hospital where I pick up my dose. He's a good old boy in his quiet, crew-cut way. I'll miss the women in the ER who always say, "Good morning, Eric," so nicely and offer me cups of coffee even though they know why I'm there. Yeah . . . I'll miss the routine.

But mostly, by God, I'm gonna miss the methadone. And then, of course, there's him.

I can feel him out there, beginning to moan and gnash his putrid teeth; Grendel waking from his long narcosis. Soon he will be outside my door, tearing with his terrible claws, beckoning me. I can hear his devilish howl, very faint, very far away, like the roaring sound one hears in the dead silence of night.

Grendel isn't just mine; he's been around since the beginning of time, since the Creation. But monsters don't just pop up, emerge fully grown out of the misty fens of the north. Even Jesus had an earthly mother, and Grendel had an earthly father. He is the son of Cain.

And Cain knew his wife and she conceived and bore Enoch. Enoch then begot Irad who begot Mehujael who begot Methusael who begot Lemech. Lemech took two wives and between them they produced all the tent dwellers, cattle herders, and harp and organ players. One of Lemech's children was Noah, and Noah and his three sons were the only people to make it through the flood. They were good old boys too, or at lest Yahweh thought so. But one of the boys turned out to have some of the maladaptive characteristics of his great-great-great-great-grandfather Cain. His name was Ham and his descendants were damned by the Lord because they were as bad as the guys He had destroyed in the flood. Evil had managed to slip through the deluge along with the various pairs of animals. Ham begot this one who begot that one who begot someone else over the centuries—and as a result there are still bad people today. People like Unferth, King Hrothgar's friend, who thought Grendel was beautiful. People like Fast Joey. People like Vlad Tepes.

But Grendel isn't a child of Ham. No—he was sired by the old man himself. After Cain finished begetting his progeny he left the land of Nod on the east of Eden and made his way north to the shores of Daneland, there to bear his guilt in private. But Grendel's spectral mother sought him out in the frozen north. She who has existed since before the Creation, before God Himself. She went looking for this most evil of all men, seduced him, and bore the miserable wretch Grendel, whose lot it was to be evil and despised, virtually invincible, and yet corporeal and mortal so that he didn't even have the satisfaction of terrorizing without fear of death as a demon does.

The legend of Beowulf is, of course, a story. No such hero ever existed. Grendel is still out there, still talking to the night, still hungry. I can feel the tingle of his nearness to me.

In six days I will be taking my last dose of methadone. The early withdrawal symptoms are worsening.

In four days I will take my last dose. I may already be drinking blank Kool-Aid with a little something to imitate the taste of methadone.

In three days it will be over. My Brother's House will be at an end and I will move on to the House of Blue Lights.

Today I took my second-to-last dose. My bone marrow is on fire and the hoary claws of the monster Grendel have pierced the armor of my soul. He has me once again . . . I believe, once more, the words I have uttered so many times before.

"I'll just do it this once," I say to myself. "Just get loaded today; then I won't do it again." They are Grendel's words, and yet, impossibly, I believe them without hesitation.

*

South Seattle Floral Supply opens at 9:00. I am parked outside, watching the window, at 8:10. As each thought of what I am doing enters my mind, I dismiss it with practiced facility. "Just this once," I insist, "just this once." Time drags. I smoke five cigarettes. I cringe with the embarrassment that is to come. I have bought scores of dried poppy pods at this place without ever offering a plausible explanation for what I do with them. The sales clerk thinks I am insane.

It will take ten excruciating minutes to complete the sale; ten minutes of her writing out the receipt, all the while stealing secret, incredulous glances at me. I will then jump into the car and drive two blocks to the Seven-Eleven store, where I will buy a sixteen-ounce Coke. I will then get back in the car, whip onto the freeway, and head north. It is an hour's drive. There is no way to make tea while riding in the car and waiting an hour is out of the question, so I've trained myself to eat the pods whole. It's not easy. The first time I tried it, I threw up. But I've mastered it, finally.

It will take the entire hour to eat the thirty or forty pods necessary to get me off. I'll pop each pod in my mouth, crunch and chew it a while, then swallow the harsh mash with a chaser of Coke. I'll finish consuming the bunch about the time I cross the Skagit County line. Then I'll wait; only a few minutes before the telltale signs begin to appear. I'll know it's beginning to take effect because a wave of nausea will come over me. I'll feel a pressure begin to build which will seem like I'm about to throw up. Instead I'll sneeze four times. The nausea will wane. My mind will begin to wander off drugs and onto pleasant topics. I will feel good.

9:02—the store opens.

"Well . . . hi, uh . . . how are you?" The sales clerk Kelly does not remember my name. She knows me only as "the Poppy Man." She gives me her usual enigmatic look, tinged with a mild revulsion and curiosity. "Back for more?"

"Yep," I say, trying to make it sound like buying dried poppy pods every few days was the most common thing on earth. "We just got a contract to do some dried arrangements for Del Monico's Restaurant in Port Townsend. It's a good deal for our business."

"You guys must really like the way these poppies look in your arrangements," says Kelly and gives me a look that says, dried-flower arrangements my ass, but what in God's name *do* you do with all these poppies?

Another customer is watching our transaction and says, "I got a friend who grows those things; he says he eats them, gets high on them."

I feign a mortified look. "Eats them? You're kidding! He *eats* them? That's crazy. They're not opium poppies, are they? They wouldn't grow around here."

The other customer laughs and elbows his companion. "I've heard of stranger things," he says.

"Is that what you do with them?" Kelly asks me. "You eat them? Yuck."

"That's ludicrous," I say, blushing absurdly. "Nobody could eat those things." But the idea has been planted in her mind. No other explanation comes this close to making sense. She gives me an even more amazed look. "Well, *I* don't care what you do with them as long as you keep buying them here." She hands me my receipt and gives me a forced smile. "See you soon," she says, and I cringe.

But an hour and a half later I don't give a shit. Kelly can think what she wants. She can drop dead. I'll never go back there again anyway, so who cares what she thinks. Fuck her.

I start eating pods in south Seattle and keep at it until I start to feel the effects at about Tulalip. Slowly but surely, my bone marrow stops burning, the tickle in my throat eases off, and I begin to glow like a mercury lamp in thick fog. The opium creeps over me with the feeling of a heavy snow falling, gently, silently, blanketing all the rough edges of my secret world. The smells, the chills, the desperate hopelessness of early withdrawal flickers and fades. I feel like a freshly baked loaf of bread. Radio station KVI (Seattle's "classic" rock 'n' roll station) plays the songs that, years ago, made me dream.

The first time you smoke weed, or drop acid, or shoot coke, or even guzzle whiskey, you experience something completely new, enter a realm you've never been in before—but opium is different. Even the first time, the experience is old and familiar, like reliving your seventh birthday.

Ah, opium: that first cup of coffee on a crisp, fall morning, those cool, light sheets on freshly showered legs, that delicate fragrance of a rose in candlelight, the warmth of down on a snowy day. Opium—so kind and gentle, so loving. Kelly has no idea what she has just sold me, nor does she know that I would happily pay her ten times as much as she charges.

Forty-eight hours later I am back again buying more. I'm off and running.

By the time I have been high for three or four days I begin to wonder why I was so worried about kicking. "It'll be easy," I say to myself. "I can do it; it won't be so hard." As long as South Seattle Floral Supply has poppies I feel confident I could quit "anytime."

This, remember, from a guy who has spent the better part of seventeen years strung out.

Incredible.

"I'm sorry," says Kelly, finally. "We sold our last bunches a few minutes ago. We should have more in a week or two."

A week or two . . . a year or two . . . a century or two . . . it's all the same. If I don't have some now, today, my world will fall apart. And that miserable bitch sold my poppies to somebody else.

*

Everybody knows that Grendel's father Cain did something unconscionable; that he killed his brother and as punishment was condemned by God—all of which makes him sound like a very bad person indeed. But a careful reading of Genesis 4 suggests there was more to it than simply a bad guy getting his just deserts.

See, Cain's parents had their problems with God, too. It wasn't just Cain. I suspect God was already keeping an eye on this first family. Anyway, when Adam and Eve's sons grew up, Cain became a tiller of the land and Abel became a shepherd of flocks. In those days God liked to have things sacrificed to Him—who knows why; he just did. The idea was to give as sacrifice the most desirable thing possible. Abel brought Him a sacrifice from his flock, probably a nice, succulent leg of lamb. And Cain brought

Him a sacrifice from his fields, maybe a sheaf or two of barley. God tended to be pretty anthropomorphic in those days, so it is not so surprising that a leg of lamb pleased Him and a bowl of barley was . . . well even God preferred roast lamb to barley gruel. But He was a just God and told Cain, "Your sacrifice may not have been all that great, but you can still be a good servant if you choose to—just as Abel is." But Cain's feelings were hurt and his nose was out of joint. You can't really blame him. Each gave what he had. How was Cain supposed to know God preferred meat to vegetables? So he rose up against his brother and slew him.

This really pissed God off.

"What hast thou done?" wailed God. "Thy brother's blood crieth to me from the ground."

So Cain became a fugitive and a vagabond, wandering around with his mark on him, gradually moving north as he succumbed to the beckoning lure of Grendel's mother.

★

I walk briskly out of South Seattle Floral Supply, Grendel screaming in my ear, "Try Wong's Florist in Lynnwood; try Wild Rose Floral in Mill Creek; try Weed's, Etc. in Edmonds." A cold rain is drizzling on me in typical Seattle fashion. A chilly wind is blowing. "Try the emergency room at Virginia Mason Hospital," whispers Grendel. "Describe the symptoms of shingles; get yourself some percodan." A seagull passes; its lonely call echoes in my head. I get into the car and begin to drive, but can't decide where to go. All the places Grendel has suggested seem so far away. I begin to weep.

Health and Treatment Services Northwest is on the seventh floor of the Cabrini Towers Medical Building. It seems like a long ride up. Others in the elevator look at me in my rain-soaked jacket and wet, plastered-down hair. I must be quite a sight. What would they say? Something the cat dragged in? Something the cat threw up? I steady myself with a hand on the wall and fix my eyes on the floor. I've made my decision. No more florists. No more midnight raids on gardens. No more stories to doctors. No more cough syrup. I'm tired—and I've had enough.

Fuck Grendel.

"Eric, what are you doing here?" asks LaWanda. "You don't have an appointment today."

"I know," I say, "but I got trouble. Any chance of seeing Cindy?"

LaWanda gives me a knowing look, filled with pathos. She's been around. She knows what the "trouble" is. "They're all in a meeting, Eric, but they should be finishing up soon. You can wait a while if you like and I can ask her if she'll see you."

I ease myself into a waiting room chair, as if I might break if I move too fast. I leaf through an old copy of *People* magazine. My damp hair and jacket smell of stale cigarette smoke. My left leg aches miserably. Sitting still is difficult.

Fuck you, Grendel, you mindless old monster. I am not insane. If I go to Lynnwood or Mill Creek or Edmonds I will only get fixed for a few days, then it is back to the House of Mirrors. I may have been strung out like a motherfucker for years, but something, some whisper of tenacity, has kept me from slipping back into illegal drug use. Something has kept me going to work. Some hint of humanness has held my family together. And the only chance I have to build on that bit of strength is right here at Health and Treatment Services Northwest.

"Okay," says LaWanda. "You can go in now." I toss the magazine back on the table and lift myself wearily out of the chair. I walk across the waiting room and into the hall. LaWanda catches me gently by the arm. "Eric," she says, "Norm's in there with them."

John Normanson is an old friend. I have known that he is the executive director of this agency, that he and I would eventually come face to face. It was because of my friendship with Norm that I was given special permission to pick up my dose in Skagit County. Norm pulled strings for me, broke rules for me, saw to it I got special treatment, and yet we have not spoken since I began treatment. What he knows of my current condition he has heard from Cindy and Dave.

John Normanson says he is called Norm because "a 'John' is a toilet." I don't know what the real reason is. Maybe he's got some sort of past he wants to separate himself from. He's the most energetic man I've ever known—the type who likes to talk on two telephones at the same time. He must work out a lot; his gut is flat and hard as concrete; his arms bulge like the Incredible Hulk. Norm's hair has begun to grey, and forms a thin crescent around the shiny, black dome of his head. He still greets people by grabbing their thumbs, but other than that there is little of the Philadelphia ghetto left in him. Norm, like me, like Cindy, has a master's degree in social work from the University of Washington. We are birds of a feather. He has been in drug treatment for years and watched every "ex-addict" he knows relapse. This is all old hat to Norm.

Cindy and Dave are sitting in chairs. Norm is behind the desk. All three are wearing the same expression: terrible disappointment. I sit down and hang my head.

"What happened?" asks Cindy cryptically.

"I didn't make it," I reply inanely. I had prepared quite a nice little speech, but somehow words fail me. I had not expected them to look so . . . annoyed. I had expected sympathy, compassion. These three are looking at me like I've done something *bad* rather than something for which I should be pitied. "It's like I couldn't stop myself," I say. "Like there was some kind of monster controlling me and all I could do was sit back and watch myself go."

"How long?" Cindy asks.

"Few weeks."

Cindy, Dave, and Norm look at each other, trying to decide who will go first. Each of them has a nice little speech too. "Well," says Dave, finally, "we always knew that inpatient care was a possibility. You've been strung out a long time. Maybe it was unrealistic on our part to think we could detox you as an outpatient. You're slick, you're a professional, you know all the ropes. Maybe it was just unrealistic."

"Yeah," I say. "Maybe so."

"There's an excellent inpatient facility in Oakland run by Dave Smith and Don Wesson," Dave says. "It's the kind of place you need – real state-of-the-art."

"Oakland?!!" I say, horrified.

"Eric," says Cindy. "You're a tough case . . . a real tough case. Drugs don't cost you any money to speak of; they don't really disrupt your life very much. That makes it difficult for you to hang on to your desire to quit. The other people we see here are literally killing themselves, dying, or else bankrupting themselves. But you, you're living a basically normal life – at least on the outside you are. It's going to take more than methadone and weekly counseling sessions to break up your pattern."

"That's right," says Dave. "There's really no alternative." I close my eyes and in my mind's eye see Rose and Adam running to leap in my arms as I arrive home from work. I feel the softness of Sarah's hand as she strokes my face in the morning, telling me it's time to get up. In the eight years since Adam was born we have never spent a night apart. Rose and Adam have been to a babysitter exactly twice in their lives. I try to imagine Sarah bringing in the strawberry crop alone or balancing the books without me. The idea of going off to Oakland for a month or two is simply out of the question.

"There *is* an alternative, Dave," I say. "There's permanent maintenance. If I can't quit I can at least spend the rest of my life on methadone. That's better than going on as I have been, isn't it?"

"I suppose it is," says Dave. "But I'd hate to see you do that."

"Why not go to Oakland?" Cindy asks. "Your insurance would pay most of it."

"Because I'm not going to leave my family that long," I say. "And besides, you know as well as I do it wouldn't work anyway. I'm a lifer. I'm a dyed-in-the-wool dope fiend. I'll never quit. There're a certain number of people in this world who can't live without narcotics, right? People who simply must have methadone?"

"That's right," Cindy has to agree.

"Well," I say. "I'm one of them. I've blown out my endorphin production system. I'll never be a normal person again. I know that, you know that, we all know it. So let's just admit it and start me back on methadone."

"Well," says Dave. "You'll need Norm's authorization for that. I can give you methadone for three days. After that it's up to Norm."

John Normanson, MSW, workout freak and old friend, Philadelphia street urchin and executive director, has been studying his fingernails the whole time. All three of us now turn to him, but Norm is in no hurry to say his piece. He reaches into his pants pocket, pulls out a nail clipper, and trims his thumb carefully. He then repockets the clipper and studies his work thoughtfully. He recrosses his legs and draws and expels a deep breath. He looks directly at me. "I agree you don't need to go to Oakland," Norm says at last, and I breathe a sigh of relief, assuming he agrees with my assessment of myself. I am wrong. "What you need is for somebody to get behind you and give you a good hard kick in the ass."

All three of us are slightly stunned. "Then after they've given you one kick they should give you another and another, til you don't know whether to shit or go blind." He stops talking but continues to stare directly at me.

"Norm, I just think that . . ."

"You don't know how to think!" Norm roars, cutting me off. "All you know how to do is take dope. You haven't had a thought in your head for years about anything except dope."

"That's not entirely true, Norm," I mumble tentatively.

"You waltz in here without an appointment, looking like death warmed over, and get the attention of the whole staff," Norm says. "We make all kinds of exceptions for you, treat you special, and what do you do? You fuck up. Then you come in here asking for maintenance. You know you haven't even paid your bill for a month? You want all this extra stuff and you haven't even paid your bill. You must be a good three hundred bucks behind."

"Hasn't the insurance company . . .?"

"And another thing," Norm continues. "Why hasn't your wife been coming in for counseling with you? You trying to do all this behind her back? You trying to kick in your spare time, huh?" Norm rages on, talking mean, acting mad. He calls me all kinds of terrible names, accuses me of things I haven't done, purposely misinterprets things I say, keeps claiming I am on his "shit list." But now I understand. Norm is using a technique known in the business as "tough love." He figures that niceness has not worked on me so he is trying a different approach. He's trying to make me mad—break me out of self-pity. Good old Norm.

"You want back on methadone?" Norm says, "Okay. I'll authorize it. But you're gonna have to jump through some hoops, homeboy. You're gonna have to show me you're worth it. Now—are you ready to agree to anything I say?"

"Of course," I say. "What choice do I have?"

"None," says Norm, "so listen up. First: You pay your bill and maintain a credit, so you're always a week ahead. No more getting in arrears with us. Next: You bring Sarah with you to every counseling session. Third: You agree to a 'greymail' contract."

"What's that?" I ask. "What's greymail?"

"It's an agreement that falls just a little short of blackmail," says Norm. "Here's how it works. You write a letter to your boss telling her you're a drug addict who has gone out of control. You date it and sign it. Then the very first time your urine test shows that you've used an unauthorized drug, I will mail it."

I think about my supervisor, Nora Gillman: intolerant, judgmental. She has never liked me. Nora herself has an alcohol problem, and like the pot calling the kettle black, she becomes apoplectic at the very thought of drug abuse. If she received such a letter I could kiss my credibility, and therefore my job, goodbye. It would destroy me. "I can't agree to that, Norm," I whine. "The stakes are too high. Losing my job would not only shaft me, it would shaft Sarah and the kids, too. I can't agree to it."

"Then it's no deal," says Norm.

"God in heaven, man . . ." I begin, but stop short. Of course . . . of course . . . the stakes are too high. I would never risk doing such a thing to Rose and Adam. If I agree to this I will keep the agreement. Nothing on earth, man or monster, could get me to use drugs again if I know that such a letter would be sent to Nora. It's an extreme measure, but it will work. I'm not insane. I won't hurt them.

"I agree to it, Norm," I say. And God help me, I write the letter.

"Okay," Norm says. "Go downstairs, pick up your dose, and go home. You've got a lot of things to think about." I slip my coat on and wipe away the tears that have again appeared in my eyes. I run a hand through my plastered-down hair, which has finally begun to dry. I walk to the door. "Eric," Norm calls as I step through to the hall. "We're not going to give up on you. I will authorize sixty more days; that's it. You ain't *never* going on maintenance."

8

The Gateway

Thirty-six-year-old Duane Sweeney stood in the shower and looked down at his pale, flaccid two hundred and six pounds. It had been a long time since anybody had called him "Skinny Jimmy." The water stung his sensitive skin, forcing him to adjust the pressure down. Duane stuck his head under the nozzle, then lathered what was left of his stringy hair with shampoo. It was the damned hepatitis, he thought to himself; that's what made his hair fall out. Now that he was finally over it his hair should be growing in thick again. Duane looked at his pallid arms as the suds ran over them. He hated the way his arms looked. Once lean and heavily veined, they now looked more like a woman's arms. The needle track marks had long since cleared, and for that he was grateful, but the years of puncturing his arms with dull needles had caused the collapse of all his surface veins.

Duane Sweeney felt like hell. It was 2:30 in the afternoon and he had just gotten out of bed. His head throbbed with hangover from drinking M-D 20/20 all night with the guys down on First and Pike, and his insides ached from the undiagnosed cirrhosis that would eventually cause his death.

"Buncha assholes," mumbled Duane as he thought of the skid row bums he had taken to hanging out with. Duane hated Seattle. He hated the rain and he hated the miserable, squalid

Morrison Hotel where he lived. In fact the only good thing about life Duane could think of was that at least he was no longer strung out on heroin; at least he had kicked that.

The shower water suddenly turned icy cold and Duane leapt from the stall cursing. He pulled a damp towel from the rack and began to dry himself off. "Now how the hell could this towel still be wet?" he wondered, knowing he had not showered for at least a week. "Goddamn, fucking Seattle," he murmured as he dressed quickly in the same clothes he had just taken off, the same ones he had slept in. Duane had felt damp ever since he arrived in the Northwest and he was damn sick of it.

If it hadn't been for Dancer, Duane would still be in San Francisco doing good. Dancer had been busted for possession with intent to distribute; then, in an attempt to save his stupid ass, Dancer had fingered Duane as his supplier. Duane had been picked up, released on his personal recognizance, and then split for Seattle. He could never go back to San Francisco now. Since then he hadn't gotten the breaks.

And beside, ever since he left the Bay Area, the Environmental Control Police had begun to hound him.

Duane had come to Seattle a couple of years ago . . . three, four years ago . . . how many years? "Let's see," he mused. "It was '71 or '72 . . . Jesus, thirteen years ago." He was about twenty-three when he arrived. He was sick so he went to the Center for Addiction Services and got on methadone maintenance. That lasted a couple of years before they threw him off the program, just because his counselor had it in for him. The asshole had said that Duane had been coming in for his dose drunk. They gave him a twenty-one-day detox and threw him out in the street. Duane had gotten a room at the Union Gospel Mission. That's when they started. Duane had been just sitting in his room, had been sitting there for three or four days, when he suddenly realized that somehow he had been given the secret of the cosmos. Duane wasn't immediately sure of the source of the information, but assumed it came from God. In a flash of understanding, he knew that he was the One foretold in Revelation.

It didn't take long for the Environmental Control Police to discover that he had this vital information, and they wanted it. Duane had become afraid to leave his room for fear they would get him.

"Come out of there, Sweeney," the majordomo for the Control Police instructed. "You can't escape us. We want information, you hear? Information. Give it to us or we'll rip your balls off and feed them to the rats; we'll scrape your flesh off with a potato peeler and pour hydrochloric acid on your exposed nerves. We can do anything, and we *will* do anything until you tell us what we want to know."

"Well what the fuck do you want to know?" Duane screamed. "I'll tell you; what is it?"

"We want information," the Minister of Agony said. "You will give us information or we will torture you and eventually kill you."

"What information?" Duane moaned. "What do you want?"

"Information," the Minister droned. "We want information . . . information . . . information."

It had been that way for years now. Duane could no longer hustle like in the old days. He couldn't even think any more. He walked the streets, carrying around the terrible burden of knowing that he and only he knew the forbidden secrets of the universe, and the Environmental Control Police were liable to turn up anywhere. And when they did, it took all of Duane's energies just to stay one step ahead of them.

Duane returned the towel to his rack in the shower room and walked down the hall to his room. The door was open. He didn't remember leaving the door open. "I wonder," thought Duane. "Are they in there?" He gave the door a gentle nudge and looked around inside. There didn't seem to be any evidence of an intruder. He checked the old mail carrier's sack he used to keep his few possessions in; it appeared untouched. He checked his shoes. He checked his coat. Nothing. He opened his one drawer where he kept his Bible, a pack of condoms, and the gardening trowel he kept as a weapon. Again, nothing. Duane walked over to his bed: a bare mattress on which he slept in a sleeping bag.

He sat down feeling a little less nervous. Maybe he *had* left the door unlocked. He put his hand on the sleeping bag and suddenly went icy with fear.

The bag was wet.

Duane leapt to his feet in terror. They had been here! He ran his hands quickly over his clothing and realized that the front of his trousers and his undershorts were soaked in urine. Some son-of-a-bitch Control Police had pissed on him in his sleep. Duane took several deep breaths, trying to control fear, slow his racing heart. This had happened many times before. They would sneak in his room at night and piss on him. In the morning he would wake up soaked. They did it just to hassle him, just to remind him that they watched his every move and could get to him no matter where he was. Duane realized once again that he could never be safe, not in this solar system.

"We've had enough, Sweeney," the majordomo for the Environmental Control Police said. "We're tired of fucking around with you. Now we're going to get rid of you. You're garbage anyway. The universe will be better off without you. Better kiss your ugly ass good-bye."

Duane trembled with fear. He knew the Control Police had tremendous power, that they could control his every movement. He knew his time was up.

"What do you want to know?" Duane wailed. "I'll tell you! Please! I don't want to die!"

"Stop your miserable whining," the Chancellor of Assassinations said, "and go over and open the window."

Duane obeyed, knowing he was preparing to die.

"Now get out on the ledge," the voice said.

Again Duane obeyed.

"Okay you disgusting piece of shit, jump out of here and let's be rid of you once and for all."

"Please," Duane begged. "Please!"

"Jump, asshole—jump!"

Duane leaned forward, closed his eyes, and tumbled headlong into the fires of hell he knew awaited him when he hit the pavement.

Intake summary: Duane James Sweeney
DOB: 8/12/48

Patient was admitted through the emergency room on a 72-hour emergency detention order as gravely disabled and a danger to self. He had jumped from a fourth-floor window of a downtown hotel, apparently responding to internal stimuli. Fortunately for the patient, he fell on an elderly woman resident of the area who, in turn, fell onto several shopping bags she was carrying. Both parties suffered minor contusions to the extremities, but neither was seriously injured. Police on the scene summoned the Designated Mental Health Professional for King County, who evaluated the patient and found him to be floridly psychotic. He was suffering from a mental disorder characterized by fixed paranoid delusions and was basically incoherent, rambling on about something he referred to as the "Environmental Control Police." In his delusional system these persecutory beings instructed him to take his own life. A check of Mr. Sweeney's hotel accommodations revealed a squalid setting, which included a urine-soaked bed and large piles of human feces in the corners of the room. There was no evidence of the presence of any food and it is assumed the patient has not eaten in some time. Bottles of psychiatric medication were found in the room, the dates on which revealed they were filled some months ago and yet the bottles were full, suggesting that Mr. Sweeney has not been taking his medication. His clothing was ragged and also urine-soaked, though his skin and hair were incongruously clean and freshly scrubbed. His dental hygiene was noted to be extremely poor. Physical exam was basically within normal limits, though there was enlargement of the liver on palpation and hepatic function tests have been ordered along with the normal battery. Mental status exam revealed a blunted affect with rambling, incoherent speech. He admitted to command auditory hallucinations of an extremely demeaning nature which he admits he is powerless to ignore. He was unable to abstract, showing very concrete interpretation of proverbs. His insight is minimal, judgment is severely impaired.

Impression: Schizophrenic, paranoid type; chronic, in acute exacerbation
Alcoholism, episodic, by history R/O alcoholic hepatitis

Plan: Admit to 8C, return to court for fourteen-day commitment and consider transfer to Western State Hospital for further evaluation and treatment. Begin Prolixin Decanoate I.M. 2cc stat and 2cc q1wk, Cogentin 1mg bid, Taractan 50–100 mg HS prn.

Elvard I. Dalsig, MD
Psychiatry Resident

"Time to draw some blood," said the nurse. "You know the routine." Duane looked in the direction of the voice. He saw two eyes, a nose, a mouth, cheeks . . . but the parts wouldn't come together. He felt bone tired and unable to bring the parts together. Eyes, nose, mouth . . . together they must mean something, but Duane could find no awareness in himself of any concept like "face."

"Come on, Duane," said the nurse, a big, friendly fellow named Lamar Washington. "I've drawn blood from you a half dozen times over the last year or so. You know me. We're friends. C'mon buddy, roll 'er up."

Duane heard words, familiar words, words he recognized; but they were just words. He was dimly aware of the fact that the words should fit together in some way, but they didn't. He looked blankly at the nurse. Without knowing exactly why, Duane realized he was not afraid of these sounds. They were familiar sounds. He was drawn to the sounds. Duane let the pieces of himself attach to these comforting sounds: a piece of him to a piece of sound.

"Environ pol, go for show . . . sleep now," Duane said in the direction of the comforting sounds, and knew immediately that what he had said made no sense whatsoever. He wanted to tell the sounds to keep coming, that they protected him. He began to cry.

"That's good, buddy," said Lamar. "You have a good cry. You been hurt pretty bad, now you go right ahead and cry. I'm here with you—I ain't goin' nowhere."

Words, words, words . . . the words kept coming. Duane took the sounds and rode on them. Something was happening in one part of him, but he didn't care. He just kept listening to the words. He saw three different tubes fill with blood from his arm. Still he listened to the words. He wanted to reach out and touch them, but he didn't know how. He knew there was a way, but he couldn't remember. Goddamn the Environmental Control Police. Duane concentrated on the sounds, and as he did, a sound of his own began working its way into his consciousness. What was it? What? There . . . no . . . there. What?

"Lamar," Duane whispered, and the effort exhausted him.

He slept.

When Duane awoke he lay still for several long minutes, taking stock of his situation. He didn't hear any voices; he didn't feel damp. The smell of clean sheets and dirty feet came to him. He knew he was in a bed. Tentatively, fearfully, he opened one eye and looked around. He saw a wall, curtains, a dresser; he saw an unmade bed next to his which was empty. He saw acoustical tiles on the ceiling.

"I'm in the hospital," thought Duane.

He took stock of his body. His feet were down there at the ends of his legs, crossed at the ankle. He was lying on his side. His left arm was on top of the blanket, bent at the elbow, hand on the pillow near his face. His right arm was . . .

"Jesus Christ," Duane thought in panic. "My right arm's gone."

There was no feeling past his right shoulder. It was gone. The ECP must have cut it off.

Duane held very still. It seemed odd that he felt no pain. "Blood," he thought. "There should be blood. If they got my arm there should be blood all over the place." Without moving Duane trained his eyes as far right as they could go. He saw the pillow, part of the sheet, a hand.

A *right* hand; *his* hand. Wha . . . ? There was a hand, a wrist, and part of a pale, unveined forearm there, sticking out from behind the pillow.

"Fucking arm's asleep," Duane thought rolling onto his back. He pulled the arm out from under the pillow and flexed his fingers. "That was close," he said aloud. "That was real damn close. They almost got me that time."

Duane tasted the putrid "cotton mouth" of high doses of psychiatric medication. His neck was stiff; his tongue felt too large for his mouth. He knew that if he stood up too quickly he would swoon, so he righted himself slowly, in stages. When he had himself in a sitting position, legs over the side of the bed, he rested. Duane listened. Still no voices. He held his head by placing a fist against each cheek and an elbow on each knee. The floor seemed to be moving, flowing, as if he were standing in a creek watching water gush between his feet. Tiny spots blinked in the periphery of his vision.

Duane knew he was in a hospital, but he wasn't sure which one; and it really didn't matter. The Environmental Control Police could not get to him in the hospital. Sure, they had their spies here. His roommate was probably an ECP spy; otherwise why would he have left his bed unmade? But while he was hospitalized Duane knew he was safe. Swaying slightly, Duane stood and made his way across the room, through the door, and into the hall. He walked to the door of the glassed-in nursing station and caught the attention of Lamar Washington. Lamar set down the chart he was reading and walked over to Duane.

"Hey man," said Duane. "When do I get outa here?"

★

"I'm Bill Eisenberg," the younger man said to Duane. "Come on in and sit down. I'll be your doctor on this hospitalization."

"What happened to Dr. Murphy?" asked Duane.

"Dr. Murphy's over at Adult Psych," said Eisenberg. "She's a resident like me. We rotate around to different places."

"How come?" asked Duane.

"Oh . . . you know," said Eisenberg. "So we get a wide range of experience."

"You're *learning* to be doctors," said Duane.

"Yeah, sort of," said Eisenberg. "I mean, no. We're already doctors; we're learning to be psychiatrists."

"And I'm your guinea pig, right?" said Duane.

"Come on Duane," said Eisenberg, pinching the bridge of his nose. "I've had this I'm-your-guinea-pig conversation too many times this week. I'm sick of it. If you'd rather talk to Lamar go ahead. If you want to talk with me, let's cut the bullshit."

Duane laughed. "Okay doc," he said. "What was your name again?'"

"Bill Eisenberg."

"Okay Dr. Bill," said Duane.

"Please," the younger man said. "Either 'Bill' or 'Dr. Eisenberg,' but for God's sake not 'Dr. Bill.' "

Again Duane laughed. He liked this guy. He had been disappointed that Dr. Murphy was gone, but this Eisenberg seemed alright. Duane still had trouble getting used to the fact that his doctors were now substantially younger than he. Bill Eisenberg was obviously not yet thirty. "I gotta get my shit together pretty soon," Duane thought, "otherwise I'm gonna end up a back ward funny."

"All right, Duane," said Eisenberg. "I've been reviewing your previous records and it doesn't take a Sigmund Freud to figure out what the trouble is. You've been hospitalized a bunch of times, but each time you go right back out to the same situation that you came out of. You keep repeating the same mistakes and you wonder why you keep getting the same results?"

"It's the Environmental Con . . . " Duane began, but Eisenberg cut him off with a wave of his hand.

"No . . . I don't want to hear about that," said Eisenberg. "I want to talk about the future, not the past."

"What do you mean future?" asked Duane, sensing that Eisenberg had something on his mind. "The future is back to the Morrison Hotel."

"To repeat the same mistakes," asked Eisenberg, "and end up back in the hospital again in three months?"

"You got a better idea?" asked Duane, knowing that Eisenberg did, indeed, have an idea. Duane was ready. He was tired of bouncing back and forth between the hospital and the Morrison.

"Well," said Eisenberg. "There's this program up north called the Gateway. I've heard good things about it. Apparently they give you a job that pays reasonable money, and they have counseling and medication and all that good stuff. I called up there this morning and they have a bed free. Want to go up and at least take a look and talk with the social worker?"

"Just to look? And talk?" asked Duane nervously. He didn't

want to commit himself until he knew a whole hell of a lot more about this place.

"That's right," said Eisenberg. "I made an appointment for you. You can ride up on the bus in the morning and be back by afternoon."

"And who do I ask for?" asked Duane.

"Let's see," said Eisenberg. "I wrote his name down. It was a funny one. Let's see . . . here it is . . . Jesus, how do you pronounce this? Deetzer? I dunno. Just show this piece of paper to somebody when you get there."

★

They didn't put me back in My Brother's House. They restarted me on a lousy thirty milligrams and have been detoxing me slowly. That first night was pure hell; I didn't sleep. It takes a good forty-eight hours to adjust to methadone when your body really wants opium. I lay there in bed, jerking and sweating all night, keeping Sarah awake. The next day I had to go to work.

Jesus.

I figured I could sort of hide in my office all day. I only had one interview scheduled, but it was a disturbing interview and I ended up walking the halls and grounds afterward, trying to get it off my mind. The patient I saw turned out to be a guy I had known years and years ago, back in San Francisco. I hadn't known him too well and, back then, I hadn't liked him at all. I liked him all right today, and I felt for him. We'd started out the same: upper-middle-class thrill-seekers playing with fire. I came out of the nether world despite my continued addiction; he stayed in. The poor bastard's as schizophrenic as hell.

I didn't recognize him when I opened the door. "You Mr. Detzer?" he asked.

"Eric Detzer. You're Duane Sweeney?"

He didn't move, just stood there grinning stupidly. I motioned for him to come in, but he wouldn't. I offered my hand to shake, but he just kept grinning. I was tired. My head ached. I figured he was hallucinating, and I damn well didn't feel like dealing with it. I ran my hand over my forehead trying to decide what to do.

"Hey . . . Easy Eric!" he said, and I felt like a horse had just kicked me in the solar plexus.

Nobody had called me that in over thirteen years.

I stared at him for what seemed like minutes, but no recognition came. "Who *are* you?" I asked at last.

"Yeah, well . . . I know I put on some weight man," he said. "It's me . . . Skinny Jimmy . . . from North Beach."

Skinny Jimmy. Jesus.

Duane sat across the desk from me and scanned the office leisurely. He seemed far more relaxed than I. "Looks like you're doin' good, man," he said. "That your wife and kids in the picture?" I swallowed drily, nodded. "Nice," he said. "Wow . . . look at those diplomas. Those yours, man? Yeah? Real nice, man, real nice." Duane lit a hand-rolled cigarette, crossed his legs, and leaned back in his chair. He picked absently at an eruption on his face. "I been clean too, you know," said Duane. "Been clean for years. I'd be doin' good too, except that some people have been hassling me."

"What people?" I asked.

"Just some people," he said, studying his shoes. "Not very nice people. I don't wanna talk about it." And I could tell by his tone of voice that Duane was not being coy. He did *not* want to talk about it. I also had interviewed enough paranoid people to know that wild horses couldn't stop him from talking about it. I braced myself. "You don't know what it's like out there now, man," he said. "It's not like the old days; it's not like San Francisco. You're up here with your little farm and your kids. You don't know what it's like."

Duane was wrong, of course. I *do* know what it's like, for him as well as for me.

Duane's physician father gave up on him years ago, but his mother, a part-time editor for a small-town weekly, still holds out some hope. It is she who answers my letter saying that they had toyed with the idea of attending the annual American Urology Association's convention in Seattle. ("The trip's tax deductible.") They will come up and talk with me. They will visit Duane, but they will not take him back to Terra Haute with them.

Duane's father sits across the desk from me, nervous and uncomfortable. Duane has described him to me as a "prick doctor." Mrs. Sweeney is on the verge of tears. "I'm glad you could come," I say.

"I want you to understand something," says Dr. Sweeney. "Duane picked his own path years ago. It was his decision to blow his mind on drugs. He knew the risks involved. That boy tested out with an IQ of 141 in the eleventh grade, one hundred and forty-one. He knew the consequences of his choice; now he has to pay the piper. He's thirty-six years old; we can no longer be responsible for him."

"The records indicate that Duane doesn't use drugs any more," I say, "hasn't used them for years."

"That may be," says Dr. Sweeney, "but the damage has been done."

I don't think Dr. Sweeney is a "prick doctor." I think he is a miserable, tortured man who, in his heart of hearts, believes he is responsible for Duane's problems. "Dr. Sweeney," I say, "we're not seeing the effects of drug abuse here. Your son is schizophrenic."

"But didn't the drugs cause that?" asks Mrs. Sweeney. "I mean, we're not just talking about marijuana. For years Duane used any drug he could get his hands on. He was even addicted to heroin. A human brain can't stand that kind of punishment. It's sure to take a terrible toll."

I look at them for a moment, sadly. "I'd like to share something personal with you two," I say. "Duane and I knew each other years ago. We ran in the same circles, used the same drugs, even shared the same needles. Duane's drug history is no more extensive than my own." In fact not nearly *as* extensive, I think. "You see, Duane's illness was probably beginning way back in high school. He was attracted to the hippies because his strange thoughts didn't seem strange to them. The fact that he hallucinated even without drugs was nothing to them. Later, the narcotics he took, first heroin and then methadone, probably served to control his psychotic symptoms. In point of fact the drugs didn't *cause* his illness; they probably masked it until he stopped."

"Mr. Detzer," says Dr. Sweeney. "I appreciate your candor. But it's a well-established medical fact that drug abuse causes brain damage."

"Duane's not brain damaged," I say. "Not in the sense you mean. He's schizophrenic."

"So what caused that?" asks Mrs. Sweeney. "What made him schizophrenic?"

"We don't know," I say. "But we do know this: drug abuse doesn't cause it, parenting practices don't cause it, and moral turpitude doesn't cause it. Maybe it's a virus, maybe a genetic problem . . . who the hell knows. Schizophrenia is a condition in which the limbic system of the brain goes out of whack. Maybe other areas are affected too. The result is a fragmentation of the personality with all kinds of behavioral sequelae, but still it is a physiological condition as much as cancer or diabetes. There's no cure, but we do have drugs to control the most troublesome symptoms and programs, like this one, to train people in ways to live with their illness. But I want you to understand something clearly: The problems that Duane has are way beyond his ability to cope with on his own. His condition is not his fault."

"And us," Mrs. Sweeney whispers tearfully, "it's not our fault either?"

"No," I say, "it's not your fault either."

The Sweeneys will return to Terra Haute and will be happy with the progress Duane will make at the Gateway program. Our parents usually are. Duane will probably be truly happy here for the first time in many years. After a year or so he will move out to a group home and maybe work in a sheltered workshop. He will go to a community mental health center for medications. He'll get his shit together.

And me? Will I get my shit together?

I wonder.

9

Death Chants, Breakdowns, and Military Waltzes

Do I like spring? The days are longer, warmer. The swallows are back and the snow geese are gone. The tulips are up and the rains are heavy. It's spring, but is spring something I like? I don't know.

This is terrible. Everything smells bad. I can't wake up and I can't get to sleep. I'm tired as hell all the time. I don't remember how to work and I don't remember how to play.

Twenty-one days. I've been off methadone for twenty-one days.

Jesus.

What do I like? There must be something. I've been strung out for so long I don't know any more. Let's see . . . what?

Opium. I like opium; that's for sure. But it's poisoning me so I don't want to use it any more. So, what else?

Hmmm . . .

I like water. Not water that falls from the sky in such obscene quantities as in the Northwest, but I do like water. I like it cool and crisp in my mouth when I'm thirsty. I like the way it cleans the dirt off my hands. I like the feel of hot water gushing around my body when I sit in the tub; it is the only thing that stops the pain of the House of Mirrors, however temporarily. Yeah . . . I do like water.

I like kids. I think. No . . . that's not true. Adam's little friend Brian drives me nuts half the time. I like *my* kids. Just knowing that they're in the next room cheers me up. I like their mother, too, but some of the time I think she doesn't like me, so that doesn't count. But I do like my kids.

This is getting a little easier. Let's see . . .

I like automatic transmission. I like clean socks. I like coffee. I like roses. I like wall-to-wall carpeting. I like movies.

I like music.

Yeah, music. When I'm using stuff I don't give a damn about music, but the minute I start kicking I really like to hear tunes that match my mood. Junkies are always reminiscing, and I'm no different. When I'm in the House of Blue Lights I want to hear the old songs again. I remember that there used to be this guy who did solo instrumentals. His guitar sounded like it was made of old coffee cans, strung with baling wire, and played inside an empty metal dumpster. I can't remember his name, but I liked his stuff a lot. I wish I could hear him play right now. Somehow his horrid, metallic sound would really hit the spot tonight. What the hell was his name? Farley? I can't remember. On one album he billed himself as Blind Joe Death, but I'm pretty sure that wasn't his real name.

Ahh . . . the old songs, reminding me of the time when life was so much more complex. Good days. Days filled with mystery and anguish, and every now and then, joy. The drug addict's world is, above all, dull. Time is divided into two categories: time spent loaded and time spent sick. The loaded time is pleasant and the sick time is unpleasant, but each leads inexorably to the other.

God in heaven! Why do I not feel better? It's been three fucking weeks!!!

The first week they prescribed some tranquilizers to help me sleep. Yuck. They gave me nightmares and made me wake up with a horrible sense of doom. And yet, when they were gone I craved more. For two or three nights I lay awake till after three, and during the days I dragged around like the ghost of Jacob

Marley in *A Christmas Carol.* I'm sleeping better now, which is some progress—I guess.

I know what the problem is: It's now the end of April. In a little over a month the poppies will start coming up. And I know where every patch is, from Tacoma to the Canadian border.

Jesus H. Christ.

★

"Your urine's dirty." Cindy's voice sounded tired and irritable over the phone. I had been off methadone for two weeks at that time.

"What?!!" I said.

"Your urine test," she said. "I just got the report back from the lab. There were traces of morphine in your last specimen. You're using again, aren't you?"

"No," I replied inanely, and though it was the truth it sounded like a lie.

"You remember the letter you wrote?" asked Cindy, "the greymail contract?"

"Now wait a minute, Cindy . . . " I began, but she cut me off.

"Can you come down to Seattle to see me?" asked Cindy. "This really isn't something we should be discussing on the phone. Can you come down tomorrow?"

"No, I can't," I said. "I've got Admissions Committee tomorrow and Utilization Review Committee on Monday. I can't get down there until Tuesday."

"Well, come down on Tuesday then," said Cindy. "I won't take any action until after I've talked to you."

"I'm not using, Cindy," I said.

"Yeah, well . . . we'll discuss it on Tuesday," she said.

Cindy's call had surprised me, but to tell the truth I didn't worry about it at first. I'd been around urine tests long enough to know that labs occasionally make mistakes. I knew I hadn't used anything. I just didn't worry about it. I figured that as long as I continued to be clean the whole thing would blow over. Then something happened, which plunged me into four days of increasing anxiety that almost pushed me over the brink. Sarah got sick.

At first it was just a cold, but it hung on and on and eventually became a sinus infection. She took erythromycin, but that didn't knock it out. Finally she could bear it no longer and her doctor gave her a stronger antibiotic and a prescription for codeine. Now, when I'm strung out, a few codeine don't even tempt me, but when I've been clean a couple of weeks, and my tolerance is down, and Grendel is screaming "just this once" in my ear, then I'm vulnerable. The first night she had them I lay awake until after midnight. I knew they were in there, just sitting in the kitchen cabinet. I tried thinking about other things, but my mind kept returning to them. The next day I could barely stand being in the same room with Sarah, knowing she was under the influence of them. She wasn't loaded. She took them just as they were prescribed. As a matter of fact, they didn't even control her pain. But I went nuts.

And then a very strange thing happened: As I drooled and salivated over a few lousy codeine, I began to worry about the greymail contract.

I didn't take any of Sarah's stupid codeine, but I did become obsessed with the idea that Cindy would not believe that the dirty urine was an error. After all, the contract said that the letter to my boss Nora would be sent if I showed a dirty. It made no provisions for errors. These kinds of contingency contracts must be adhered to rigidly if they are to be effective. What if Cindy sent that letter? Nora would jump at the chance to get some of the administrative heat off her by putting it on me. She would insist that I go for inpatient treatment and Health and Treatment Services Northwest would go along with her.

I didn't sleep well the next night. Who would support Sarah and the kids while I went into the hospital for a month or two? I knew I had used up all my vacation and sick leave, and had no money at all in savings. Who would pay for the hospitalization? My insurance would cover about half. How could I go back to working at the Gateway program after my secret was out? Rural Washington is not ready for a social worker addicted to narcotics.

My credibility would be destroyed. Where would I work if I lost my job at the Gateway? I was scared . . . really scared.

But why? I didn't do anything! All I had done was go three weeks without opium, a two-year record. Why should I go through all this fuss and worry over something I hadn't done? It wasn't fair. I began to get mad as hell at Cindy and Norm and Dave and Ted. "I've had it with those assholes," I thought. "I've been doctored and counseled to death!" The madder I got, the more I worried. By Monday I was convinced Cindy was going to send the letter.

But Tuesday came and went without a hitch. Cindy's been at this a while. She could tell by my coloring, my voice, my general demeanor that I was not strung out again. I left another urine specimen which she sent to a different lab. It came back clean. Oddly, I had the same feeling that I get when I talk a pharmacist into an extra refill, the feeling of having gotten away with something.

"Okay," said Cindy, "you've convinced me. Now my job is to convince Dave and Norm."

Two days later Nora Gillman called me into her office. "I was sorry as hell to hear about your problem, Eric," she said.

"What problem is that?" I asked, genuinely baffled. Nora looked at me like I was crazy.

"Well, I got this letter from you . . . " she said, holding a sheet of paper in her hand with my writing on it. "Didn't you write this?"

Jesus Christ.

My peripheral vision faded as I zeroed in on the letter. Yes, I had written it. And now it was coming back to destroy me. I couldn't believe they had sent it without warning me. I guess they just didn't believe me. Images from my eighteen years of drug addiction flooded my mind: smoking weed and dropping acid with my high school buddies, pills and potions in college, Johnny, Fast Joey, the hospital, the poppies—things with poison in them.

I made a snap decision.

Before Nora could say anything more I reached under my shirt and depressed the subcutaneous button on my back. This deactivated my cloaking device, causing my human look to evaporate and returning my face to the normal reptilian features of the planet Xlotan. Nora blanched as I flicked my forked tongue at her and hissed. Withdrawing my communicator from the pouch under my neck, I hailed the ship.

"Commander Yzz, this is Earth operative 0059. I have contracted a Terran disease which is apparently progressive and fatal. It has caused me to blow my cover. Quickly—beam me aboard."

I gave Nora a jaunty little wave as my molecules began dissembling and traveling up the transporter beam. Good-bye Earth, you miserable, dank, smelly planet. I'm going home.

"Eric," said Nora. "Eric, are you all right? You look like you're about to faint."

"I'm okay," I said. "I was just sort of hoping the ground would open up and swallow me."

"I can imagine," said Nora, smiling. "I can just imagine."

★

I think I understand the story of Cain and Abel now. It's not so complicated really. To our modern ears, God's reaction to Cain seems unfair and reprehensible, but to the ancient Hebrews it probably made perfect sense. See, they were a shepherding people. They may have raised a little of this and a little of that, but primarily they were shepherds. If God made man in His image, then God too was a shepherd. Cain knew it, and God knew he knew it. All the minute details on how to prepare offerings to the Lord are laid out later in the Scriptures, but one thing certainly went without saying: When you make a sacrifice to a shepherd's God, you sacrifice an animal. You don't offer up fruits, grains, or vegetables. Cain knew perfectly well God wouldn't like his sacrifice, but he did it anyway.

We're all descended from Cain and it seems many of us inherited this tendency toward recalcitrance. There are some things God allows, some He prohibits, and some He doesn't care about one way or the other. He doesn't want us to kill our brothers, He doesn't want us to be too smart, and He doesn't want us to take opium in large quantities. It's obvious. Isn't it?

*

"She what?!!" screamed Sarah.

"She sent the letter," I said. "She let me believe she wasn't going to and then she did."

"But you said it was a mistake," moaned Sarah.

"It *was* a mistake," I said.

"Jesus Christ," said Sarah. "Jesus motherfucking Christ almighty! Now what do we do? How are we going to live if you lose that job? I'm not going to go back to living like animals again—not ever again. Fuck, why did you write that goddamn letter? I knew it was a fucking mistake. Jesus Christ." Sarah kept raving. I let her vent. Eventually she calmed down.

"You know, Nora was really pretty decent about it," I said. "I don't think she's going to make a lot of trouble for me. I mean, it would sort of be the pot calling the kettle black."

Boom chucka chucka chucka . . . boom chucka chucka chucka . . . I can hear old whatsisname banging on his awful metallic guitar, a harsh, tinny breakdown.

*

It has now been four weeks.

Now five weeks.

So where is this wonderful feeling of freedom ex-dope-fiends talk about? Where is the euphoric rush that is supposed to follow the breaking of the narcotic stranglehold? Why am I not kicking up my heels in ecstasy? I feel no different today than I did a month ago.

In a matter of weeks it will be the Season. The little plants are already three or four inches high. I found one in my garden. I pulled it up and threw it away, but there are tens of thousands more out there, getting bigger and bigger. Soon I'll see them everywhere. What do I do then? I won't be able to resist. I know myself; I won't be able to resist. What I need right now is a miracle.

★

Duane's dead.

I found him myself. Dallas, the head counselor, called me in my office. "Hey, your boy didn't show up at his assigned workshop again."

"Whadaya mean . . . Duane?" I asked.

"That's right," said Dallas. "Old Skinny Jimmy's still in the rack. He's been complaining of a stomachache for the last couple days. I put him on the list to see the doctor, but this isn't the first time he hasn't shown up for work. Do you think maybe you could go down there and try to roust his ass out of bed?"

"I'll get him up," I said. I left my office without the slightest sense of anything being wrong. I walked past the staff station and on to the living area. I knocked on Duane's door: no answer. I opened the door slowly and peeked in. There he was, in his underwear, lying crosswise on the bed, his feet hanging over one side, his face down, and one arm extended across the other side.

"Duane," I said. "Wake up. Time for work." When he didn't answer I put my hand on his shoulder, intending to shake him awake. The second I touched him I knew. He was cold as ice. I wanted to run; I wanted to vomit; I wanted to weep. It took considerable effort to roll his great bulk over and, when I did, I saw something I will never forget. His right arm, which had been hanging over the bed, stood straight up in the air. Rigor mortis. Jesus.

The coroner called it death by accidental overdose. Somehow Duane had gotten hold of a dozen quaaludes. When that poison hit his cirrhotic liver, he never had a chance. Now he's dead. Just when he was finally doing good.

Boom chucka chucka chucka. Boom chucka chucka chucka.

★

"So," said Ted Schimmle. "You must be feeling pretty good: six weeks clean. That must be some sort of record for you.

"Yeah, I feel okay," I said.

"Well, I have to admit I was expecting a tad more enthusiasm," said Ted. "A year ago you couldn't go more than seventy-two hours. Why so glum?"

"The Season is almost here," I said. "You know me. Do you really think I can stop myself when the opium starts blooming?"

"Yes, I do," said Ted.

"Well, you're wrong."

Ted shifted in his chair. He seemed to have lost some weight since the last time I had seen him. I noticed that he no longer smoked cigarettes. "What do you think it would take to keep you clean?" he asked.

"Nothing short of a miracle, Ted," I replied. "You got one?"

"Maybe," said Ted. "Maybe I got one." I could tell that Ted had something in mind, but I couldn't imagine what. Nobody knew more about the treatment of drug addiction than I do. I felt certain that there was nothing I hadn't already thought of. I was wrong.

"You ever heard of naltrexone?" asked Ted.

Naltrexone. The miracle drug. Yes, I had heard of it: the long-acting narcotic antagonist that had been used experimentally for ten years. Naltrexone. Just the sound of the name sent shivers down my spine. A junkie on naltrexone can shoot three hundred dollars worth of heroin and not feel a thing. It blocks the effects of narcotics. Naltrexone. How often had I prayed to a God I didn't even believe in to let me get hold of naltrexone?

"Forget it, Ted," I said. "The FDA has that stuff tied up. There's no way they'd let you dispense it to me."

"Ah . . . you're getting out of touch, Eric," Ted said. "They released it for general use two weeks ago."

Incredible. I got my miracle. Beowulf may not have needed a sword, but I do. With naltrexone I can slay the demon. Let the Season begin!

Weeeeee're off to see the wizard . . .

10

The Poppy Thief

"Roll up your sleeve," said Dave Taber, "and let's go ahead and do it." I had come back to Health and Treatment Services Northwest for a "narcan challenge," a necessary precursor to taking naltrexone. The Skagit Mental Health Center had said they were not set up to do it. When I went in, I was genuinely clean and ready to take on Grendel with my chemical sword. I had stopped methadone in March and gone virtually the whole month without narcotics.

Narcan is a very short-acting narcotic antagonist. It's like naltrexone, except that the effect wears off in about twenty minutes. If you give a hooked addict naltrexone, he is immediately catapulted into Stage Four withdrawal for forty-eight to seventy-two hours, and that is a medical emergency. Incredible as it may seem, some dope fiends practice such massive denial that they are even able to convince *themselves*—and thus their doctors—that they are not strung out. So narcan tests whether or not you are clean, without jeopardizing your life. The narcan challenge is a good idea—but it was not necessary in my case.

Dave slid the needle into my vein, pulled back on the plunger to be sure he was in, and then emptied the one-cubic-centimeter syringe into my bloodstream. "Here," he said, placing a cotton ball on the puncture wound. "Hold this."

"How long does it take?" I asked.

"About ninety seconds," said Dave, replacing the cap on the needle, then throwing the whole outfit into a special box. We were silent a moment.

"If I had been strung out," I asked, throwing away the cotton, "how would I have reacted?"

Dave chuckled. "Well, first you would have thrown up on me. Then you probably would have rolled up in a fetal position on the floor and jerked around in clonic spasms. You'd have shit in your pants and sweated like a pig. You know the picture."

Yeah . . . I know the picture. Jesus.

Cindy came into the exam room as I was rolling down my sleeve. "Hey stranger," she said, so nicely. "How've you been?" Cindy, eight months pregnant, was big as a house.

"Oh – I'm okay," I said. "You know – not good, not bad."

"I guess you passed the challenge," said Cindy.

"Yeah, I passed," I said. "It's interesting, you know; today's April 12. It was April 12, 1971, that I was discharged from Maricopa County Hospital after my very first detox: fourteen years ago."

"Well," said Cindy. "Happy anniversary." She sat down near my chair, a puzzled expression on her face. "Hey – is something wrong? You seem more down than I would have expected."

I felt uncomfortable with Cindy's closeness to me, and unable to think of anything to say. I, too, had expected to feel better after nearly two months of abstinence. "It's just . . . you know . . . it's hard: harder than I thought it would be. I feel sort of . . . I don't know . . . tired I guess." My fingers were dancing their little dance.

"Are you seeing Ted?" asked Cindy.

"I've seen him a few times," I said. "My employer is requiring me to continue with him."

"Are they requiring anything else?" she asked.

"A bunch of things," I said. "I have to fill out daily itineraries, submitted in advance. I have to see Ted. I have to take naltrexone, supervised by a pharmacist. I have to arrange for progress reports from the mental health center. I'm also not allowed to keep the company car overnight any more."

"The company car?" asked Cindy. "Why not?"

"Beats me," I said, smiling. "That one baffles me. I think Nora has always suspected me of misusing it."

"Have you?" asked Cindy.

"Once," I said. "It was just after I started working there. I got reported by a citizen who saw me pick some flowers."

"Poppies?"

"Of course," I said. "I haven't misused the car since then, but Nora will never believe it. Anyway—it's not so inconvenient for me. It's the agency that suffers. When I'm on the road it means I have nearly two hours less time to work."

"They're trying to be helpful," said Dave, "be helpful to you and protect the agency at the same time. You can't expect them to be right on the mark every time." Dave pulled some pamphlets out of a drawer and passed them over to me. "Here's all the information we have on naltrexone," he said. "Read it and if you have any questions you can call. I better warn you, though; not a lot is known about the stuff, and to be perfectly frank, this is the first time I've prescribed it. I don't have any personal experience with it."

★

I should have known, that very first day, that naltrexone would not turn out to be the miracle I was expecting. I should have known, because that day I got loaded again . . . with a script for one hundred naltrexone still in my pocket. I decided to do it . . . just one last time.

I stopped at a florist in Edmonds. I swallowed my embarrassment. I walked up to the door and turned the handle. Shit.

It was locked. A sign in the window said: Closed Sunday and Monday. It was Monday. Shit.

Now, I have never in my life had an extrasensory perception. In fact, I have never believed anybody who has claimed to have had one. But that day in Edmonds, standing on the porch of Weeds, Etc., I swear to God a voice inside my head spoke to me.

"The back door is unlocked," it said.

And indeed it was.

What if I had been caught? My car was parked right out front—the license plate clearly visible. It was a bright sunny day. There were people around. What if somebody had seen me? I was guilty of breaking and entering, burglary. What if I had been seen? I certainly would have lost my job—gotten myself in serious hot water. And for what? . . . six bucks worth of *papaver somniferum*.

It flipped me out that I would do such a thing. So the next day I decided to start naltrexone. Jesus. I got so sick I couldn't believe it. I spent the day snapping at the kids, and spent the night jerking and sweating. I felt okay the next day, but forty-eight hours after my first dose I took a second. Wham! Sick, snap, jerk, sweat—shit. It was terrible.

Eventually I got used to it, though. I took it and I did fine. I took it for a couple of months and I stayed clean. I took it and took it, until finally it seemed crazy to take it any more. So I stopped.

I don't even remember, offhand, what the issue was that caused me to start using opium again. Maybe I was upset about something . . . maybe I was afraid of something . . . who knows? Maybe I had just gotten overwhelmed by the everyday hassles of life. It doesn't make any difference, really. It's always something.

Beowulf was right . . . swords are fucking useless.

*

Anyway, I'm off and running. Another year another Jones, repeating the same mistakes. I really thought I had it licked this time. Four clean months.

It's harder this year. In the first place, it has to be a complete secret. Once again, I have to hide it from Sarah. That means no growing my own, no going out at night, no using the blender to make it into a tea. I have to steal them in broad daylight and eat the pods whole. Also, I have a lot of competition this year. Other people have discovered my secret. I drive past yard after yard that has been picked clean: from Tacoma to the Canadian border.

I'm getting caught in the act a lot. It used to be I could go up to the front doors and ask the ladies if I could have them. Ninety-nine times out of a hundred they'd say yes. No more, though. Between me and the other pod heads, everybody who grows poppies ornamentally has had them stolen. It infuriates them (as it did me when so many of mine were stolen last year). Yesterday a guy actually called me at home. His *neighbor* had seen me steal poppies. He took down my license plate number and got my number from the DMV. Jesus he was mad.

"What's in those poppies anyway?" he asked, "some kinda dope?"

"No, no . . . of course not," I said. "I just wanted the dried pods. My wife uses them in her flower arrangements. I'm really sorry about this. I figured you wouldn't want them."

"Do you make a habit of just taking things out of people's yards?" he asked angrily.

"Look, I'm sorry," I said. "I'll be happy to pay you for them if you like."

"You come around my place one more time and I'll show you how you're gonna pay!" He slammed the phone down.

My skin was crawling with embarrassment.

People think that yards and gardens are so nice and sweet and good. Bullshit. They're full of poison. Around here we get a lot of deadly nightshade with its lethal red berries. We have *amanita moscara,* which is hallucinogenic and toxic. Cows and horses drop dead from tansy ragwort.

Cultivated plants are just as bad. The delicate little sweet pea can make a real mess of a person's insides. And our own state flower, the rhododendron, is death on the bloom. In fact, the rhody's cousin, the azalea, has a proud history of killing indirectly. Around 400 B.C. an army of Greek soldiers camped by the Black Sea and ate honey made from the nectar of the Pontic azalea. They were massacred by their enemies because they were too sick to hold a sword. Three hundred years later the same thing happened to an army of Romans in the same spot.

Gardens can be deadly places; flowers can be lethal.

*

"Hey . . . ," said the burly guy in the yellow pickup, "hey you! . . . Hey!! What the hell do you think you're doing!!!"

Driving around, driving around, driving around. Stop and jump, jump and grab, grab and run.

"Did somebody say you could have those flowers, buddy?" snapped the bleached blonde housewife.

"What are you doing in my yard? Just what in the world do you think you are doing?!!"

Driving around . . . driving around . . .

Fifteen pods from the house on Highway 20, eleven from the church flower bed, five each from the alley and the place on Jennings Drive. Not enough, but better than nothing.

"Hey you! *Hey!!!*"

The leaves are starting to turn again. The maples are yellowing and the alders are reddening. The cucumbers are almost over, though the cauliflower are still going strong. All the wheat has been combined and stored. Sarah is harvesting the garlic: her final crop of the year. We'll slaughter the cows in a few weeks—and that will be the end of the Season. August is gone for another year.

Christ . . . how could I have done this again? How did I let myself get strung out another time? I was doing so well.

So what do I do now? How do I kick this new habit? And how do I do it in a way that will be different from all the other times? How do I take on Grendel without repeating the same mistakes? Obviously methadone isn't the answer, nor is naltrexone. Ted isn't the answer, and neither is Cindy. Narcotics Anonymous is a good organization, but I'm just not that into it. Sarah? . . . what can she do? Other than bite her lip, roll her eyes, and moan, "mo-ther-fuck-er!!! . . . not again!" And going to Nora would only result in my finally being fired.

No—no person, no medication, no program is going to be of any help. The only way to kick a Jones is to stop taking drugs. Just stop . . . suffer through the Blue Lights and come out on the other side.

It's funny, you know; I don't even have a name for the House that comes next.

★

Aletha Mann slowly peeled off her gardening gloves and dropped them on the kitchen table. A morning of weeding had started her arthritis acting up. Now she would be in pain the rest of the day. Aletha rubbed the knobby knuckles against the side of her face, noticing again how soft her wrinkled skin felt.

"I'm old," she thought. "Old and alone."

She gingerly picked up the bunch of cosmos she had brought in and stuck it in a vase. Then she carried the vase over to the sink, filled it with water, and set it on the window sill. She thought about Nate, dead now nearly fifteen years.

"He was a good man," Aletha thought, "basically a good man. He could have been a good doctor, too, if the bottle hadn't sapped his will and turned him bitter." Aletha remembered the hundreds of arguments, the terrible scenes.

"Doctors can't help *anybody,*" Nate used to say. "Half the treatments we have don't do anything, and the other half make people worse. Why even bother? Why waste my time? All they really want are the painkillers anyway. Why bother with tests and X-rays and surgery. Give 'em the pills and let 'em go home. That's all they want, anyway. Give 'em the pills, I say."

The more Nate drank, the more he lost interest in his patients. The older ones died, and the younger ones found new doctors. The neighborhood began to deteriorate, but Nate didn't notice, or maybe he didn't care. Aletha would spend hours in their bedroom, crying her eyes out, while Nate snored in his boozy sleep.

He had plenty of patients. Oh yes, people still came to see Dr. Mann. And they were just what Nate wanted: people who didn't care about diagnosis or treatment, people who only wanted the pills. They were drug addicts.

Aletha took a bottle of Windex out of the cupboard and began cleaning the kitchen windows. "The old fool," she mumbled aloud. "He could have been a decent man." Aletha clenched her teeth. She hated what she called "weepy women," and no longer allowed herself to cry, even in private. While other doctors were making good incomes and having fulfilling lives, Nate was barely scraping by on what he could squeeze out of his dope fiends. Few pharmacies would fill his prescriptions, though those that would did a volume business.

When Nate was killed, Aletha felt only relief. There was no funeral. They had no friends, no children. She simply had him put in a box and put in the ground. She then left Oakland and moved as far north as she could get.

Aletha Mann stood back from the window to admire her work. She had a thing about clean windows. She looked out at her garden, at the tall, graceful gladiolas.

"Who's this now?" she said as a bright yellow Pinto wagon pulled up in front of her mobile home and parked. A nice-looking, well-dressed young man stepped out of the car and walked over to her flower beds. Aletha smiled. Yes, her flower garden was certainly worth stopping to admire.

"I wonder if I should go out and visit with him?" thought Aletha. "It would be nice to talk with somebody under seventy for once." As Aletha watched, she realized that her original guess of his age was probably off by ten years. There were lines under his eyes, and his eyes seemed red and swollen. He was probably thirty-five, but a trim, healthy thirty-five.

Aletha had just decided to go outside and greet him when the young man suddenly lurched into the flower bed, grabbed two large poppy plants that had dropped their petals, and bolted back to his car.

"Hey! Hey you!!!" Aletha yelled, banging on the window, but the door to the Pinto slammed shut and it sped away, spinning its wheels.

"Well I'll be damned," said Aletha, and dropped into a chair.

(That would be a wild coincidence, wouldn't it? Running into Dr. Mann's wife that way? Well – Dr. Mann probably did have a wife. I've often wondered what she thought about him and his specialized practice. She must have known; I wonder how it made her feel. Much like Sarah, I'll bet.)

★

It's raining again. The harvested fields are turning into great tureens of brown soup. When I stand under the fir tree out front, I hear the chatter of a thousand barn swallows. They are forming into flocks, about to begin the long migration down the western flyway. The tomatoes didn't ripen again; they never do.

I pull the car up to the curb and gaze across the street at the dried poppy plants – maybe a dozen pods. I shut off the motor. Is anybody looking out a window? Are there dogs around? I stub out my cigarette, open the door. There's a light on in the house, even though it's nearly eight in the morning. Are there people in there? Will they write down my license plate number? I cross the street and walk nonchalantly past the house. Twelve lousy pods; I need three times that many at the very least. Is it worth the risk for twelve pods? I walk past in the other direction. Now I'm looking suspicious. If anybody is watching they'll think I'm casing the place. Is that a face in the neighbor's window? Or is it a lampshade? So what if somebody yells at me? Is it going to kill me to get yelled at? Fuck 'em; let 'em yell. Yeah . . . but what if it turns out to be somebody I know who sees me? Somebody I work with?

A door slams somewhere. I turn and run back to the car. I cruise past two other places I know. One has a person standing on the porch, the other . . . well . . . it just doesn't feel right.

I'm out of time. Got to get to the office now. No more time for poppy hunting until lunch hour.

★

What if I just stopped? What if I decided: That's it, no more? What if I just suffered silently through the House of Mirrors, saying I had the flu? It hasn't been that long—just a few weeks. How bad could it be?

Could I do it? Yeah . . . I probably could. In fact, what choice do I have? Back to Cindy Olsen? You think John Normanson would authorize any more methadone? Ha! But I still need to gradually reduce my intake a bit more. When I get to the point where a dozen or so will stop withdrawal, then I can cold turkey. Another week or two should do it. If I tried to stop abruptly right now, I'd buckle and end up taking some godawful risk. Got to wait.

And God knows, after nineteen years of drug addiction, I know how to wait. I've gotten very good at it. I know how to wait and I know how to suffer. I've learned how to go through withdrawal without even showing it, which is kind of like yawning without moving your lips or jaw. Sometimes I sit on a bench in the mall, watching all the normal people. Some of them look happy, but most look hassled, angry, tired, or just blank. A lot of people have a bad day, but all of *them* can get into bed at night and think to themselves, "Yeah, but at least I'm not hooked on opium." Probably not one in ten thousand actually says that, but all of them could.

I can't.

Someday, somehow, I'm going to be clean again. I imagine I'll fight it every step of the way, but eventually I'll find myself unable to get hold of any stuff and I'll have to clean up. When I do, I'm going to make it a nightly ritual to look at myself in the mirror and say, "Yeah, but at least I'm not hooked on opium." During the weeks I spent clean recently, I kept worrying that I didn't feel "good." I was disappointed. I didn't realize what I had. So what if I didn't feel good—at least I wasn't hooked on opium.

Adam and Rose have started back to school—he in the third grade, she in kindergarten. Sarah is having her first solo show in a Pioneer Square gallery—this is her first chance to be financially fortunate in art. We've put the strawberry field to bed for the year, and laid in hay for the stock animals. Soon we'll build our first fire of the fall. The world continues to turn—I have no idea why.

11

The Open House

And so it begins.

The House of Mirrors is upon me, with all its familiar unpleasantness: the leg, the nose, the old songs. I know it so well, and yet somehow something is different this year. I can feel it in my bone marrow: the same marrow that is starting to burn. I can't quite put my finger on it, but something is definitely different.

Look at that face in the reflection there. That's me: not old Bud's youngest boy, not Rose and Adam's papa, not Sarah's husband, not Easy Eric, and not Eric Detzer, MSW. It's me. The same me who, at five years old, used to pin a bath towel around my neck and stand with fists on hips, trembling with fear, facing the darkness in the hall and challenging it to do its worst; the same me who at ten mixed my blood with the other cub scouts in the pack and swore eternal allegiance to each other; the me who at sixteen stood at the door to adulthood, so confident and yet without a clue what would come next; the same me who at twenty-two had already had a lifetime of experiences and figured there was no place to go but up, and so laid out an ambitious set of goals like college, grad school, home, family, children, career; the same me who at twenty-eight gazed at the crib of my first child, knowing I had already attained all the goals I had set, and figured there was no place to go but down. I am the same person who, a year ago, wrote myself a note that said, "You have one year to knock off this opium-eating nonsense—if you fail, you will take your own life."

It's me there in that reflection. "Hi, Eric. How are you, homeboy? You look a little tired and bedraggled. Your crow's-feet are deeper and the grey hair in your mustache is much more noticeable. I hear you're strung out again."

Maybe I need a new hero. I was thinking about the hordes of poppies that beseige me, and they're not so unlike the imperial troops of ancient Assyria who were sent by Antiochus to occupy *Ariel:* "the lion of God," Jerusalem. The Hebrews didn't have any sort of armed force, but there were guerrillas who harassed the evil empire. The toughest bunch was led by a guy named Judah who hammered away mercilessly at the occupation forces. In fact, that's what the Jews called him: Maccabee, "the Hammer." After years of skirmishing with Judah, the emperor finally got sick of it and sent his whole imperial army to crush the resistance. But Judah was not only tough, he was smart. He lured the Assyrians into an ambush and cut them down like lambs at slaughter. Jerusalem was retaken and the temple was rededicated. The single day's supply of oil for the lamps lasted eight days.

Maybe I could be Judah and Sarah, Rose, and Adam could be my Maccabees. Maybe we could drive the imperial poppy pods from our sacred farm: "the Lion of Strawberries." Maybe we could start thinking of ourselves as the Chosen People. Maybe we could fight on the side of angels.

You know, I don't think I'm going to kill myself. I know I promised I would, but I changed my mind. I mean, what would be the point? I used to think that Rose, Adam, and Sarah deserved a "real" husband and father, but lately I've been thinking that maybe I wasn't so bad after all. Ted Schimmle used to tell me that I wasn't a real junkie. I always pooh-poohed him, but maybe he was right. Real junkies don't stop their drug-seeking behavior just because it's time to go to work; they don't miss out on scoring just because their families are waiting at home. If I was a real junkie like Fast Joey I wouldn't pass through the House of

Mirrors every fall. I would take that five thousand bucks I have squirreled away in an IRA and buy heroin with it. If *I* can't get poppies, I go without drugs. That doesn't sound like a "real" junkie.

★

All my life I have taken great pride in the fact that I am descended from the real-life Dracula. When I tell people about it, they always get a big kick out of the story. But I wonder—is it really something to be proud of? Vlad Tepes, the Impaler, was an awful man; he did terrible things to people. Like once a deputation from the Turkish sultan arrived in Transylvania to discuss opening up diplomatic relations. When presented to the Count, the ambassadors bowed to him without removing their fezzes.

"Why do you insult me thus?" asked Tepes.

"Sire, it is our custom in Constantinople to leave our heads covered," replied the ambassadors. "We mean no disrespect."

"Well, it is not *our* custom," replied Tepes. He summoned guards who held the Ottoman dignitaries on the floor and nailed their fezzes to their skulls.

By the same token I have frequently been embarrassed by my profession. One time I was in the lobby of the juvenile court, waiting for the trial of a child abuser on whom I had filed a dependency petition. I was out of cigarettes, so I walked over to a group of police officers who were talking and laughing together.

"Excuse me," I said. "Any of you guys got a cigarette I could bum?"

"That depends," said one, smiling. "Are you with the prosecution or the defense?" The others chuckled.

"Prosecution," I said.

"Well then, help yourself," said the cop, extending a pack. I took one and lit it.

"So what are you?" he asked, "Lawyer? Doctor?"

I swallowed dryly. "Neither," I said. "I'm a social worker."

"Wooo-hooo!" he said and they all laughed. "If you're a social worker—give it back!"

Something is definitely screwed up. I've got my priorities all wrong. I should be embarrassed by the former, proud of the latter.

*

"How was work today?" Sarah asked as I walked into the kitchen.

"Fine," I said.

"You look kind of tired," she said. "Are you okay?"

"Sure, I'm fine," I said. "It's just taking longer to throw off this bug than I thought."

"Well if you're sick, go to a doctor," she said. Sarah was bustling around the kitchen, wiping down the counters, rattling dishes. She didn't look at me. "I was hoping to get the rest of that firewood stacked, but if you're sick . . . "

"That's okay," I said. "I can stack the wood. Just let me sit down and rest for a few minutes first."

"Why don't you get into bed?" she asked; the irritation in her voice was unmistakable.

"No, really, I'm okay," I said. "I can stack the wood."

"Well which is it?" she snapped. "Are you okay or are you sick?"

I was expecting this. When you live with a person for seventeen years you can tell when something is wrong. In the past I've always used this as my excuse for telling her. I've also always tried to tell myself that it isn't "fair" to hide it from her, that she has a *right* to know. I know better now; I'm not going to slip into that same trap.

It's been a year since I first admitted to her that my opium eating was out of control, that I was using more than she, that sometimes I was using behind her back. Since then I've twice stopped and started up again. It doesn't help to tell her; it just makes things worse. Let her think I'm tired. A person has to walk this lonesome valley alone.

*

"Hey Eric," said Carrie Maguire, one of the other social workers at the Gateway. "Have you seen Don yet this morning?"

It was after 9:00; Don was an hour late.

"I guess I haven't," I said. Don Treadway, the clinical director, was frequently late, but a full hour was unusual even for him. "Should we call him at home?" I asked. "Maybe he overslept."

At that moment I heard a raucous laughter down the hall. Don had arrived and was sharing a joke with one of his patients.

"Oh my God," said Carrie, holding her forehead, "he's got his shirt on inside out." Don was walking down the hall toward us, listing very slightly to one side. As he drew near I detected the unmistakable smell of scotch.

"Let's duck into your office," said Carrie, "before he tries talking to us."

The two of us sat down in my office. I've worked with Carrie for four years, yet she has come into my office only a dozen or so times. She sat uncomfortably on the edge of my desk for just a moment, then stood and walked over to the window. Carrie was upset.

"This place is a real loony bin," she said. "The staff are worse than the patients. Half the people who work here ought to be committed." I considered her words and realized that I didn't really know any of the people at the Gateway. I mean, I *work* with them, but I don't really know them.

"What do you mean?" I said. "Are there other alcoholics here?"

"Half the staff!" she said. "Maybe more. And the others are weird too. You know Diana? Well, Children's Protective Services has a file on her two inches thick. And Bobbie Larsen? She's been going to a shrink for years. She takes eight milligrams of xanax a day; *eight* milligrams! That's twice the maximum dose! And that guy who works in the kitchen, what's his name, Eddie Long? He lives with his mother, even though he's forty-two, because he gambles away his whole paycheck. I can't believe it, you know? I mean, what are these people doing in mental health work? Leona goes home after work, turns out the lights, and cries all evening until bedtime."

Carrie lit a cigarette, put it down in the ashtray, ran her fingers through her hair, then pulled another out of the pack and lit it. I sat silently for a moment, letting the things she had said sink in. I guess I'd never really thought about my coworkers and what they were like after 5:00.

"And Don," Carrie continued, "he's getting really out of control. Every day he comes in half an hour to forty-five minutes late; most days he reeks of booze. Have you noticed how he constantly repeats himself and says things that don't make sense? His wife once told me that he had alcohol treatment in the past, and it looks like it's catching up with him again. It's embarrassing having him as a boss."

I'd never seen Carrie in such a state. I'd thought she and Don were friends. Carrie went on raving about Don, saying that she was going to report him to the Mental Health Division director. We could hear Don laughing in the hall. Carrie rolled her eyes and stared out the window.

I didn't really want to talk about Don at all. I wanted Carrie to get out of my office so I could sit in my chair and watch the window. I felt unbearably hot and short of breath. I could see a reflection within a reflection within a reflection.

Don walked in and stubbed his toe on a chair. "Morning," he said. "Shall we get together and discuss the new Social Security regulations?" He looked terrible, five feet ten inches tall and no more than a hundred and twenty pounds. His greasy, dyed black hair stood in stark contrast to his pasty white skin. His tie, parted at the knot and extending to each armpit, made him look almost comic. He did indeed have his shirt on inside out.

"What else is there to discuss?" snapped Carrie. "We went through it all pretty thoroughly at the meeting on Friday."

"Oh . . . yeah," mumbled Don. He obviously had no memory of the discussion. He turned to me. "So, Eric—doing any *gardening* this year?" he said with a conspiratorial smirk. "Getting some nice flowers, are you?" He chuckled cruelly. I winced. Nora must have told him.

"The only ones we're raising commercially are statice," I said. "People use them in dried arrangements."

"Dried flower arrangements, huh?" he said, and laughed again.

"I've got to write a disability report," said Carrie and she started for the door. Don's laugh turned to a coughing fit, which quickly turned to a labored gasping for breath. Carrie took his arm and waited until he caught his breath. "You okay?" asked Carrie, "that sounds awful."

"No, no . . . I'm fine," said Don. "Say—did you hear about Dallas?" Don pulled a cigarette out of his pants pocket and lit it. "He was picked up by the sheriff. I guess he beat his wife pretty bad."

"I really have to go," said Carrie, but Don ignored her.

"You watch—he'll end up divorced again. Sharon won't put up with that shit any more than his first two wives would. He tries to come across so smooth and together, reading Shakespeare and Plato, then slaps his wives around."

My left leg was aching miserably, just above the knee. My insides were churning. It was all I could do to keep myself from telling Don to shut up and get out. I wanted to be alone. I wanted to suffer in private.

I wanted opium.

Carrie finally made her escape while Don was trying to pull his socks up. A patient poked her head into my office. "Mr. Detzer," she said, "could I see you?"

"Sure Eula," I said, grateful for the diversion. "Uh, Don, I need to meet with Eula."

"Yeah, okay," Don said, "but let's get together later. We need to discuss the new Social Security regulations." He lurched out of his chair and left.

"Come on in, Eula," I said. "What's up?"

Eula Spencer was twenty-five years old and had been hospitalized thirty-one times. Her speech was difficult to understand because her tongue would thrust to one side when she spoke: a symptom of tardive dyskinesia, irreversible nerve damage caused by antipsychotic medications. Her face showed no emotion: what we in the business call "flat affect."

"What can I do for you?" I asked.

"I want to leave," Eula said. "I hate it here. I want to get out."

"Well, there's nobody holding you here," I said. "You're free to leave any time. Where would you go?"

"Back to Seattle," said Eula, "get a place of my own. Anything is better than this." I knew Eula well enough to know that, even though she appeared flat, she felt things deeply. I also knew she was incapable of living on her own. Eula had always liked it at the Gateway.

"You can go," I said, "I'll help you find another place to live; but tell me, is something wrong? Did something happen?"

"Everybody hassles me all the time," said Eula. "They're always talking about me and saying that everything's my fault. I just can't take it any more."

"Who hassles you?" I asked. "Who's saying these things?" I already knew the answer to my questions, of course. The voices Eula heard condemning her were auditory hallucinations. Eula did not respond to my question. She was sick and tired of having people tell her that she "just imagined" the voices. We sat in silence a moment.

"What's wrong, Eula?" I asked at last, "What's bothering you?"

"It's this place . . ." she began, but I cut her off.

"What's eating you?"

Eula stared directly at me, unblinking. "Duane," she said softly. "I miss Duane." No trace of emotion showed on her face.

"I miss him too," I said. "I miss him very much. He was our friend – yours and mine."

"You know it's my fault he's dead," said Eula. "Everybody says so; I've heard them. That's why I've got to get out of here. How can I stay when everybody knows it's my fault?"

"How could it be your fault?" I asked. "You were his friend."

"It just was," Eula said. "I know it. I'm a bad person and it was my fault."

I knew there was no point trying to convince her that her guilt was delusional. Years ago I used to go through all kinds of verbal gymnastics in an effort to get delusional people to see reality, but all the logic and horse-sense in the world will not shake apart a fixed delusion. There was really very little I could do for Eula, other than to assure her that I myself did not think she was a bad person.

Poor Eula. Not only did she have to suffer the pain of losing her friend, she also had to bear this enormous burden of guilt. I wish I could have made her see the truth: that Duane's death was not her fault.

It was mine.

When you make a sacrifice to a shepherd's God, you sacrifice an animal: not fruits, vegetables, or grains. Old Yahweh hasn't had a human sacrificed to Him since the days when He was called Ba'al, but I sacrificed Duane. I hope He liked my sacrifice better than Cain's. And now that He has Duane, I hope He'll give me some peace.

(What am I blathering about? This is crazy talk. I didn't "sacrifice" Duane in a pagan ritual; he died from an overdose. I'm getting carried away with this Torah stuff. Must be finally losing my marbles.)

Carrie threw open the door to my office. "Eric, come here quick, it's Don." I jumped from my chair and ran out into the hall. Don was lying on his back, his face covered with vomit. The smell of scotch hung heavy in the air. Don's breathing was shallow and raspy. Other people gathered around.

"Call the aid car," I snapped at Linda, my secretary. "I think he's aspirated some vomit. Move!"

Don moaned, arched his back, and rolled over on his side. Carrie stood over him and cried softly. Eula poked her head out. "Oh my God," she said, "I've killed another one. My God, my God!"

My head was buzzing and I felt faint. Here was Don, probably in hepatic coma and certain to develop pneumonia from the vomit in his lungs. Carrie was frozen from the shock of Don's condition. And Eula was undoubtedly suicidal over her lethal "badness." Dallas, the only staff member who was really competent at emergency first aid, was in jail for wife-beating, so not available to handle the situation. What could I do? I knelt there, burning with third-stage withdrawal, and waited for the aid car.

★

You know what I wish? I wish my father had a grave. After his death he was cremated, according to his wishes. His ashes were scattered somewhere around Oak Creek in northern Arizona. There is no place, no marker, no symbol I can use to conjure up his memory. I always used to think graveyards were silly, but recently I've taken to visiting the Pleasant Ridge Cemetery and wishing that I had a special spot there where I could go and pretend to talk with him.

I've felt especially close to him lately. I know he would have understood what I've gone through, since he had the same problem with booze that I have with opium. I've always wondered if the reason why he told me the family legend about our ancestor Vlad was because he knew, even when I was a kid, that I carried "the curse." But old Bud could never help me develop a positive self-image in the face of the curse, because he had never been able to himself. He was stronger than I, though. He managed to stop drinking without changing his low opinion of himself. I couldn't.

I'd like to be able to tell him about this past year: all the pain, fear, loneliness, and despair it has brought. It was just a year ago that I sat down in his big, old chair and decided, "tonight, by God, I am going to kick." It's funny now, how I thought I could do it over a three-day weekend. I had no idea, back then, that I was headed for a Mr. Toad's wild ride through treatment programs, multiple relapses, fireworks on the job, and a close brush with suicide. I really had no idea what I had become.

It's hard to believe that this past year, 1985–86, was only twelve months long, just 365 days. When I couldn't kick over that long weekend begun in Bud's old chair, I got Ted Schimmle to refer me to Health and Treatment Services Northwest. I took methadone for a while, detoxed, relapsed, took methadone a while longer, then detoxed again in the spring. I stayed clean a little while with the help of naltrexone, but when summer (the Season) came, I stopped naltrexone and soon relapsed again. I spent much of this last summer, like the nine or ten summers before, marinating myself in opium. And I spent much of this last fall, like before, weaning myself from the poppy as the supply dwindled. Mostly, however, I've spent this past year *remembering.* All the years have begun to melt together, and I can no longer remember what happened in 1983, what happened in 1979, or what happened in 1981. I do know that I slashed my first pod in 1976, and in a couple of months from now it will be 1987. I remember this has been quite a year.

I know I feel different this year from other years. As long as my addiction was a secret, some of it even from Sarah, it seemed so much more . . . what? . . . insurmountable? Something like that. Being on methadone was a drag, shlepping myself down to Health and Treatment Services was a pain, and revealing myself to the Gateway people was a horror. But by doing those things I've found I've brought my addiction out of the realm of heroes and monsters, and exposed it for what it really is: a disease, just a simple, prosaic disease, like pneumonia or the clap. When you feel as though you're cursed, there's not much you can do about it, but when you're sick . . . well, you can throw off a sickness. And I'm beginning to feel like maybe, just maybe, I could actually lick this nonsense now.

I hated being in treatment, but I guess I have to admit that it did me some good. I had spent so many years trying to quit on my own. That was a big mistake. And every year I'd repeat the same mistake and naively expect a different result. Beowulf left his sword on the Daneland beach and tried a whole new approach to dealing with Grendel. I tried something new, too. I left my pride on the Skagit River flats and went for treatment: physician, heal thyself. I don't know . . . I just feel different. And it may be that I feel different enough to make this year be different. Maybe I can even make this year be *the* year.

Am I all wrong? Am I full of shit? I don't know. Maybe I'll start using again as soon as I find a new source of stuff. The floral supply places will soon be getting in this year's crop of dried pods. Maybe I'll start gobbling those up again. Maybe nothing's changed.

But by God I do feel different. Something about getting it out in the open where everybody can see it makes it seem so much less powerful. Like I said, much as I disliked treatment and awful as it was exposing myself at work, I think those things helped. I don't know why I should find that surprising. Mental health treatment is, after all, my profession. Why should I be surprised that it works?

I wish I could tell old Bud that looking for heroes is a futile exercise. There are no heroes. All any of us has is himself. Bud went to his grave (or his creek bed) believing that, if only he could be more like St. Francis . . .

I'd like to share with him my discovery that he and I are not the only people in the world who made mistakes. Lots of people have demons inside—maybe *everybody* does. Maybe there aren't any villains, either. Maybe Bud and I are regular Joes, no different from anybody else. Everybody knows that Gateway patients do crazy stuff, but as I look around I see that the staff do equally dysfunctional, "maladaptive" things. Dallas, Don . . . all of them. And the thing is, Gateway staff are probably a bit more together than the general population. The Gateway is a good program, run by good people. But even good people have problems. I sure would like to tell my Dad that he was a better person than most of those guys he felt inferior to. And that maybe I'm an all right person too: poison or no poison.

I've learned some things about our infamous ancestor that I wish Bud could have known. He worried about the family curse too. Uncle Vlad's last name wasn't Tepes; people didn't have last names in those days. Tepes is just old Slavonic for (what else?) "the Impaler." Vlad himself didn't use Tepes; he called himself Vladislaus Drakyula, which means: Vlad of the Order of the Dragon. He was, indeed, the ruler of Transylvania, but his title was *voevod,* which does translate to "prince" or "count," but is not an *inherited* title. A better translation would probably be "warlord." He had to fight somebody or other to get his position.

He was a bad apple, certainly, but all families have one or two bad apples. It doesn't mean that the whole family line is cursed.

Besides, there's no such thing as *moroi:* undead. There's no such thing as vampires.

★

Don was taken off to the hospital. Carrie rode with him, holding his hand and weeping softly. I kept the door to my office closed for the rest of the afternoon. I didn't want to try to answer any of the patients' inevitable questions. Eula took a PRN of taractan and went to bed.

I left early. I wanted to take a little drive before going home. Ha ha ha: "a little drive" indeed.

I headed east and north, into a part of the valley I rarely go. I turned down one back road after another, watching gardens. It happens three or four times every year: I find a new yard that hasn't been hit. I was trying to make this be one of those times. I wasn't going through any kind of internal struggle – I was just going to do it this one more time.

It didn't take long. Ten minutes after leaving the Gateway I passed a farmhouse. Between it and the barn was a garden, and in the garden were two big, beautiful poppy plants – maybe twenty-five pods to each plant. There were no close neighbors, no car parked in the driveway, and the front curtains were pulled. The day was overcast and darkening.

I parked beside a large laurel bush, which shielded me from the house. Because I was under cover I had time to give some thought to my plan of attack. I knew there would be a side window. I figured I could head directly in and hide behind a small shed. From there I would be able to see whether the side window was curtained. If it was, I could simply grab the plants and run straight back out. If it wasn't, I would continue through the garden, slip around the barn, and head back to the car from the far side.

Good plan.

I walked slowly from the road, looking up, as though I might be a birdwatcher. When I got to the shed I cautiously peeked around the edge. The window was *not* curtained, and I could see an old woman sitting at the table writing. Okay: plan B. I made my dash into the garden, heading for the poppies, but just as I was about to grab, I trod on what felt like a hose . . . or maybe a snake. It was neither. It was the tail of an old, deaf cat. She had been asleep between some tomato plants and had not heard me coming.

"Yeeee-ow!" she wailed, and my heart jumped into my mouth.

I like cats. I like cats very much. Though part of me wanted to run from the sound, another part of me wanted to go after the cat, stroke her fur and scratch her ears until her hurt and fear went away. I was torn. I took a step in the direction the cat had run, then thought better of it and took a step in the opposite direction toward the barn. I was in a state of confusion. I took another step toward the barn, turned, started toward the cat again, then turned again.

I must have been a bizarre sight: walking around in circles like that. And it didn't help my condition at all to hear the dogs begin to bark.

There were two of them: huge Samoyeds, making enough noise to wake the dead. I stopped my ridiculous little dance and stood stock still, feeling panic start to well up in me. For no particular reason I looked down at my shoes and realized they were covered with mud. How would I explain such muddy shoes to Sarah?

"I gotta get out of here," I thought, and made a dash for the barn, knocking down corn stalks and ripping my shirt on a blackberry bush in the process.

I could hear the dogs coming closer. By the time I got to the far side of the barn I figured they must be in the garden. There they apparently stopped, but continued their deafening racket.

A door slammed. "Boris? Natasha? What is it?" a woman's voice called. The dogs kept barking. I was sweating heavily and felt light-headed and unreal. I couldn't decide whether I should make a dash for the car or stay put until Boris and Natasha grew tired of playing watchdog. I stood there motionless, tense as a watch spring, but I simply could not make up my mind. All I could think of was the car; I had to get to the car. I wasn't worried about license plates, neighbors, or anything. I just wanted to get to the car.

And then I realized I could no longer hear Boris and Natasha.

"My goodness," said a voice, and I looked up into the face of eighty-two-year-old Mrs. Florence Knudsen.

I was a sight. I was covered with mud and ripped by blackberries. I was bleeding from scratches to my nose and cheek. I was caught redhanded.

"Can I help you with something?" Mrs. Knudsen asked coldly.

"I'm sorry I disturbed you," I said, blushing ridiculously. "I thought I saw a little saw-whet owl land over here. I was trying to get a closer look when the dogs startled me."

"Well, I do encourage them to bark at strangers," she said. "I would appreciate it if next time you'd come by the house and let me know what you're up to. Yesterday *and* Tuesday Boris and Natasha chased people out of the garden." Mrs. Knudsen obviously knew what I was after in her garden. There had probably been a half-dozen poppy plants to begin with, before other hop-heads got them; but Florence Knudsen wasn't one to make accusations without proof, so she let me babble a few more apologies and then leave.

I drove home feeling despondent. I was crushed that I hadn't gotten any stuff, and I was also disappointed in myself that I had tried. I'd been drug-free for several days. Another high would have set me back badly. I felt sad, that same sadness I used to feel every time I'd hear the song "Kumbaya." When I was young we used to play a lot of music. My buddies and I would get together out in the desert at night and do old blues stuff, jug band music, maybe a little bluegrass. Then, invariably, when we were taking a break, some asshole would pull out a nylon-string guitar and strum chords while singing "Kumbaya." It never failed. That song would bring everybody down, take the life out of the evening. People would start to drift away and within a few minutes the session would be over. I could never figure out how such a downer of a song, a song that would predictably make people sad, ever got to be so popular.

★

That night the phone rang at 3:00 A.M. I had only been asleep a couple of hours. "Hello," I mumbled.

"Hi, Eric," the voice at the other end said. "This is Tom: Gateway, east unit. You're on call tonight, right?"

"Am I?" I asked.

"Yep, you are," said Tom. At the Gateway the professional staff rotate on-call duty. I hadn't realized it was my week. "Sorry to wake you," Tom continued, "but we got some real trouble. I just found Howard Walker in the men's bathroom. Eric . . . he, well . . . he cut off his penis."

"Oh my God," I whispered. I'd been the on-call person for several suicide attempts, lots of assaults, and even an attempted rape. I was no novice. But this took me a while to process. "What have you done so far?" I asked.

"Standard first aid," Tom said. "Direct pressure to the bleeding while we waited for the aid car. They're just taking him out on a stretcher now. Jesus, he bled a lot."

"Were the aid car guys able to determine whether he'd cut the ephemeral artery?" I asked, snapping into my professional role.

"They didn't say," Tom said. "Why?"

"If he did, he's dead by now," I said. "If he didn't, he's got a chance. Look—it'll take me about twenty minutes to get to the hospital. I'll keep the beeper on in case you need to get hold of me. Did any of the other patients see him?"

"No," said Tom. "Everybody's still asleep."

"Okay, good," I said. "Try to get that blood out of there quick, okay?"

"Okay," said Tom. "I'll talk to you later."

I was dressed and out the door in five minutes. I pulled into the hospital parking lot at 3:24 A.M. The aid car had arrived only moments before me. I walked up to the reception area—and there I had a momentary shock. Behind the desk sat Joanne, the woman who used to give me a cup of coffee each morning when I came in to pick up my dose of methadone. Jesus, life in a small town.

"Well, hello stranger," Joanne said in a friendly voice. "What brings you here at this hour?"

"Hi Joanne," I said. "I'm the officer-of-the-day from the Gateway program. They're bringing in one of our patients with a self-inflicted wound."

"Yeccccch," Joanne said. "He's one of yours?"

"That's right," I said, "and when the medicos are through with him we're going to have to slap an ITA hold on him."

"A what?" asked Joanne.

"A . . . you know . . . a commitment, an emergency detention order," I said.

"Oh, right," Joanne said. "Well, you're in luck. The on-call shrink is already here on another case."

"Dr. Lundbeck?" I asked.

"That's right," said Joanne. This is wild, I thought. Mike Lundbeck was the psychiatrist from the Skagit Mental Health Center, the same guy who had prescribed medications for *me* when I was seeing Ted. Interestingly, I felt no embarrassment. I was into doing my job, a job I do very well, and it was almost as if that other guy, the scumbag methadone drinker, was a different person.

Time flew as I snap-stepped around like a well-oiled machine: filling out forms, making necessary phone calls, consulting with people. It was surprising to me how quickly they patched Howard up. I felt no small amount of pride when the ER physician announced that Howard was going to make it because the Gateway staff handled the situation so well and so quickly. "That must be a hell of a good program you've got," he said, and I beamed. It's true. The Gateway *is* a hell of a good program.

I got in to see Howard just as the sun was coming up. "How're you feeling, Bugsy?" I asked.

"I dunno," said Howard, "pretty woosey."

"You gave us quite a scare," I said.

"Yeah, I guess I did," said Howard. He was white as a sheet. "I'm really sorry, Eric, sorry I caused everybody so much trouble."

"I'm just glad you're okay, Bugsy," I said. "It's worth the trouble if you're okay. Now tell me – what was going on?"

"Well, you know: They said I had to cut it off so I did."

"The voices?" I asked.

"Yeah," said Howard. "They said if I didn't, everybody at the Gateway would die."

"Are you hearing the voices now?" I asked.

"A little," said Howard. "Sort of."

"Okay, Bugsy," I said, holding his shoulder. "You rest and get better. I want you to stay in the hospital a few days, okay?"

"Sure, Eric," he said. "Whatever you say."

"Good," I said. "Now – there's another guy going to come in and talk with you. His name is Mike Lundbeck, a friend of mine. He's a psychiatrist. You can be open and honest with him, okay?"

"Will you be with me?" asked Howard.

"If you like," I said. "Sure – I'll stay with you."

"Yeah, I'd like that," said Howard. "I'm kinda scared."

"I'll be with you, Bugsy," I said. "You don't need to be scared."

⋆

"You want some coffee?" Mike Lundbeck asked. We had finished with Howard, written our affidavits, and turned the matter over to the county Mental Health Professional. Our part was over. It was 9:30.

"Sure," I said. "It's too late to go back to bed. This is going to be a long day." We walked down to the cafeteria. I had coffee and cigarettes. Mike had green tea and munched on almonds.

"So, how are things with you?" Mike asked.

"Not too bad," I said, and as I uttered those words it dawned on me that they were true. For the past few hours I had honestly felt pretty good.

"I guess you got that poppy business under control, huh?"

"Well, yes and no," I said. "I've had relapses. To tell you the truth, I'm just coming out of a relapse now."

"You could have fooled me," Mike said. "You seem fine."

"Yeah, well—I'm okay, I'm past the worst of it. I really think I'm on my way out now. I *feel* different now than I've felt before."

"What's different?" asked Mike.

I gave a snort-like laugh. "I've been asking myself that same question," I said, "and I don't have a good answer. There's something about having it out in the open, somehow. When I started this nonsense ten years ago, I actually believed it wasn't really opium I was using. When I got hooked, I kept it secret. When I hid it, I lost control. By the time I came in to see Ted, it had an almost magical power.

"And now?" asked Mike.

"Well, I've spent a year in treatment. My wife knows. People at work know. *You* know, for God's sake. I couldn't have had this conversation with you a year ago.

Mike took a sip of his tea. "So where does that put you now, you know, in that scheme of yours: the House of Mirrors or what?"

"No . . . I think I'm just about through that. I'm in the House of Blue Lights now," I said.

"And how long does that go on?" Mike asked.

"Oh, Jesus . . . a long time," I said, "months and months. I don't really know . . . it's been four or five years since I actually got past the House of Blue Lights. I don't even have a name for the House that comes next."

"You should think of one," Mike said. "You can't expect to get some place unless you know where you're going."

"You got any ideas?" I asked. I'd spent some time trying to think of a good name. I suppose the reason I hadn't been able to was because I hadn't really believed it was possible to get through Blue Lights any more.

"Well, you say that the key to beating addiction is to not keep it secret," Mike said. "How about calling it the Public House?" I pondered this a moment. It was good, a nice little *double entendre,* but it didn't quite cover it.

"There's more to it than not keeping it secret," I said. "That's part of it, but not everything. What was it they used to say in graduate school? . . . necessary but not sufficient?"

"Spare me," Mike said.

"There is more to it," I said. "There's also the issue of it being an illness rather than a character flaw, a problem rather than a curse. Something reasonable. Like maybe a Real House."

"Real House . . . " said Mike. "It's a little dorky, don't you think?"

"I guess so," I admitted. I took a final sip of coffee and stubbed out my cigarette. Mike looked at me disapprovingly so I flipped him a bird and laughed. "I better be getting to work," I said. "I'll have to give this some more thought."

"Wait, I'll walk out with you," Mike said. "You know, Ted was really worried about you at one point. We even discussed the possibility of starting you on an antipsychotic medication."

"You did?!!" I asked incredulously. "Why?"

"You seemed to be getting delusional," said Mike. "Ted says you got to the point where you thought you were Dracula or something."

"Jesus, Mike," I said. "That wasn't delusional. I *am* related to the guy Bram Stoker used as the model for his novel. I never seriously thought I was Dracula, I just got into the similarity between vampires and drug addicts. Maybe I got a little carried away with it, but I was never frankly psychotic."

Mike's interest was up. "What do you mean—what similarities?"

"Well, vampires are obsessed with the substance they crave—to the exclusion of everything else. They go out at night to get it—just like me when I go out for poppies. When they get blood, they're totally satisfied. They don't need anything else: food, sex, love—anything. If they don't get blood, they die; a junkie without stuff panics like a person facing death. Blood brings life and strength to a vampire—like opium does to an addict. I don't know—I just see all kinds of parallels. And the fact that I'm honestly descended from Vlad Tepes made it that much more intriguing."

"Vampires keep their lot a secret, too," said Mike. "That fits in with your analogy. And to their neighbors and stuff they seem very charming, if a little distant—like you."

"One thing about vampires," I said. "Once they become an 'undead' they're stuck. There's no turning back. You can't reverse a curse; no amount of counseling can do that." We made our way down the hall and out into the parking lot.

"I remember you used to talk a lot about your wife and kids, and about your father," Mike said. "I was concerned because it seemed like you were wanting to quit 'for the kids' and trying to draw some kind of strength from the memory of your father. I knew you weren't going to make it, taking that tack."

I stared at Mike. He was a year or two older than I. Ten years earlier, he would have seemed hip, with his bushy hair, levis, and Mexican sandals. Now he was beginning to look anachronistic: an aging hippie, a child of the sixties, a baby boomer . . . like me. I had always considered Mike Lundbeck one of the nicest people I knew, and that impression was being confirmed again.

"You know," he said after a long moment, "if I was my ten-year-old I'd say 'Stare hard, retard.'"

I blinked and looked away. "Sorry," I said. "But you're right. That's the other thing. It's gotta be for yourself. Don't keep it secret, believe it's manageable, and do it for yourself. Does that make sense?"

"Yeah, it makes sense," Mike said.

"Hey—I've got it," I said. "The next House . . . "

"What is it?"

"The Open House."

★

Lots of people have an animal they identify with. For Rose it is the snowy owl. It's kind of her totemic image and every time she sees one she feels like the occasion is extra special. Sarah has a special attachment to certain dogs: especially her own, Bell and Jesse. Adam was born in the Chinese Year of the Dragon, which is certainly special.

I myself was born in 1948: the Year of the Rat. I always thought it was sort of disappointing to be associated with rats: They have a reputation for being mean and for carrying bubonic plague. They are friends of Uncle Vlad. But rats are really kind of admirable in ways. They are well known to be intelligent and crafty. More than that, though, they are strong and incredibly persevering, and as the *I Ching* constantly reminds us: "perseverance furthers." If a rat is tossed into a lake or something, it will tread water for three solid days. Three days!!! There's no doubt about it—in certain ways rats are worth emulating.

It'll be Thanksgiving soon. Bob and Elena are coming over. They've been thinking about getting back together. Thanksgiving will be the first time in eight months that they've broken bread at the same table. I'll be glad if they decide not to get divorced.

I went to see Don in the recovery house a couple days ago. He looks good. He's put on some weight and looks well rested. Al White, the superintendent of the Gateway, said he could have his job back as soon as he dries out, but Don has decided to take early retirement. Part of being strong is knowing when you're beaten.

That night at Florence Knudsen's was the last time I went out hunting. A few weeks ago, I carried my Dad's big old easy chair upstairs and put it in the spare room. I put his cowboy hat on the seat and his pointed boots on the floor in front of it. Now I have a little memorial I can visit whenever I feel like talking to him, though the urge to do so has become less frequent.

Sarah's art show went well. She didn't make a lot of money, but the turnout for the opening was good and her gallery has scheduled another show for next year. Sarah says she's glad I stopped poppies, but I think she's still waiting to see what happens. It's going to take a while before she lets down her guard again.

There will be another poppy season next year . . . and the next and the next. I'll have to face my obsession for the rest of my life. But maybe I've learned something this past year that will help carry me through.

I'm not looking for gods and heroes any more, and I'm not worrying about monsters and curses. I know that this obsession begins and ends with me. It's part of me – as much a part of me as my grey hairs, my crow's-feet, or my rose tattoo. I am a drug addict. I will always be a drug addict. That doesn't mean I have to use drugs, though; it only means that I will never be able to take it or leave it. I must either take it, or I must leave it. On or off, like a light bulb.

I had a friend once named Joel. He had an obsession too. Joel couldn't decide on a sexual identity. He disliked sex with girls and was attracted to boys, but he found homosexuality morally unacceptable. Joel suffered the tortures of the damned trying to resolve his conflict. He took it right to the brink of suicide. Finally, he sought counsel from a priest he admired. Father Ryan's advice to him was so direct, so simple, it almost sounds superficial. What he said was: "Don't make your problem your identity."

So that's what I'm trying to do. Though I am a dope fiend, I am also: a father, a husband, a social worker, a person. I'm a guy who has an illness . . . and when my illness kicks up, I can go to Mike or Ted or somebody and say, "I need a hand." The secret of the Sangre de Cristos can die like Uncle Vlad in the sunlight. Sometimes I think I'd like to rent a billboard on Interstate 5 that says: "Eric Detzer is a junkie, but he doesn't mean any harm."

Joel ended up converting to Catholicism, entering a seminary, and getting ordained. He's not a pastoral priest; he's in the Benedictine Order. I don't know exactly what he does, but he seems to have found peace. He followed Father Ryan's advice. Leslie Anderson, RN, used to give me similar advice back in the hospital: "If you can't handle it, baby," she used to say, "cut it loose."

In a few years I'll be forty. That means half my life is gone, but it also means I have half my life to go. I used to assume that I'd end up being an astronaut, a neurosurgeon, a professional football player, a secret agent, or a rock 'n' roll star: all young geniuses at the Verde Valley School did. It's funny, too, because I no longer *want* to be any of those things. The pay is good, but the hours are unacceptable. I don't think secret agents get to spend a lot of time with their kids. A person could do a lot worse than work in a backwoods insane asylum and raise organic strawberries on the side.

I don't know how guys in Harlem or South Philly do it. They may emerge from drug addiction, but the alternative isn't all that great either. Those who make it out must have a lot more backbone than I. I knew some of them back when I was a "real" junkie, but I don't know any now. I don't know where they go.

As for me, I'll stay right here. A year ago I said that I knew it was time to quit drugs. Since then I've gone through a lot of false starts, misdirections, and feints—looking for ways to start building my new House. I think I've got it now—and I'm ready to begin.

Ding dong, the wicked witch is deeead.